ESSENTIAL ELEMENTS

for Band

COMPREHENSIVE BAND METHOD

TIM LAUTZENHEISER • JOHN HIGGINS • CHARLES MENGHINI
PAUL LAVENDER • TOM C. RHODES • DON BIERSCHENK

To create an account, visit:
www.essentialelementsinteractive.com

Student Activation Code
E2TU-0106-6830-6928

ISBN 979-835013688-3

HAL•LEONARD®
A Muse Group Company

REVIEW

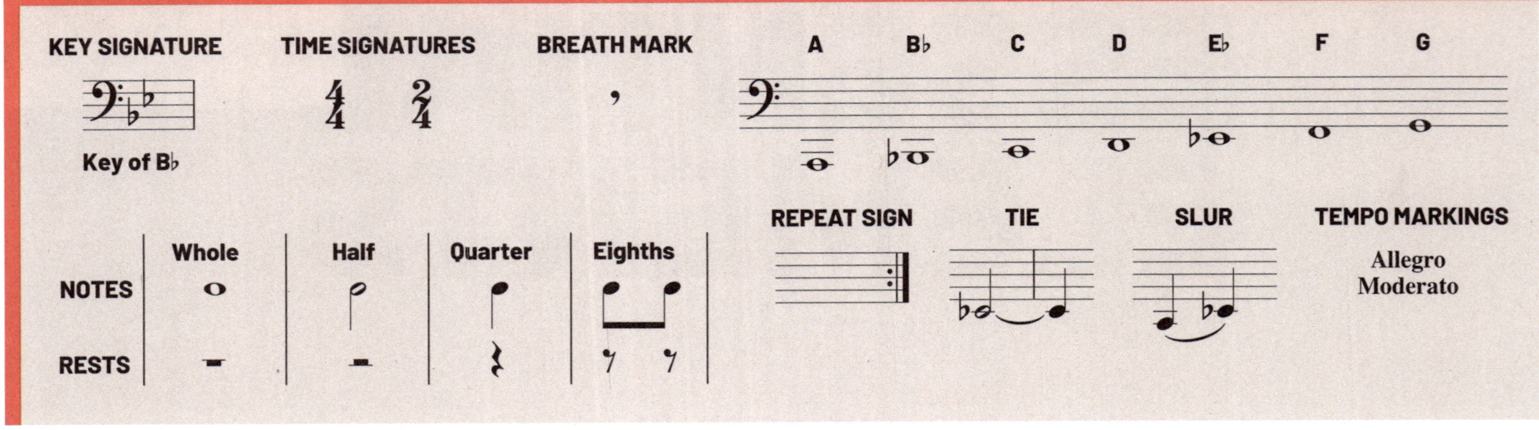

1. TECHNIQUE TRAX

2. WELCOME SONG

African Folk Song

Allegro

3. THAILAND LULLABY

Thai Folk Song

Moderato

4. SHEPHERD'S HEY

English Folk Song

Moderato

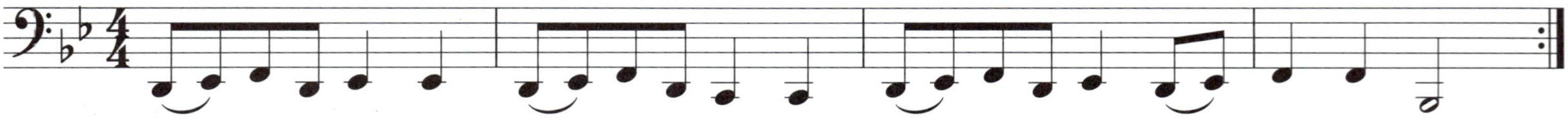

5. THE CRAWDAD SONG

American Folk Song

Allegro

REVIEW

KEY SIGNATURES

Key of E♭ Key of F

TIME SIGNATURES

3/4 C

A♭ E A♭

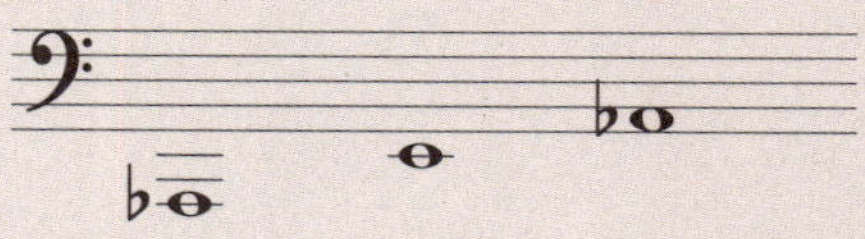

Dotted Half Note

Dotted Quarter & Eighth Notes

1st & 2nd ENDINGS

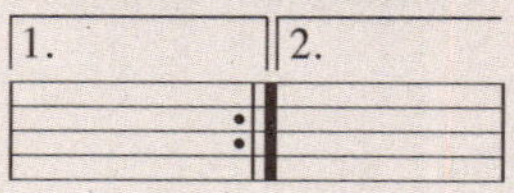

DYNAMICS

p - *mf* - *f*

PICK-UP NOTES

TEMPO MARKINGS

Andante
Maestoso

6. AMERICA/GOD SAVE THE QUEEN

Based on a Traditional Anthem

Andante

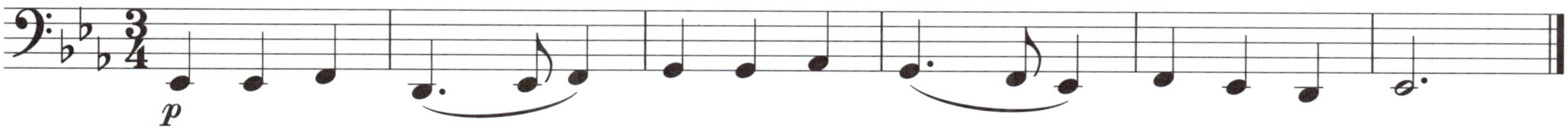

7. WEARING OF THE GREEN

Irish Folk Song

Moderato

8. ROSES FROM THE SOUTH

Johann Strauss, Jr.

Allegro

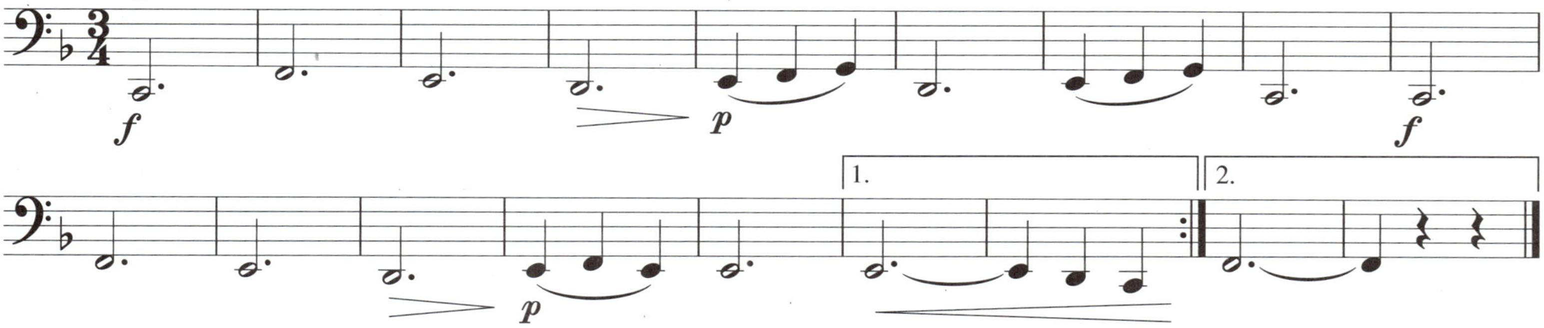

9. CRUISIN' THROUGH THE PARK

Moderato

10. TRUMPET VOLUNTARY – Duet

Jeremiah Clarke

Maestoso

REVIEW

MULTIPLE MEASURE REST 2 | **ACCENT** > | **FERMATA** | **D.C. al FINE**

A **B♭** **C**

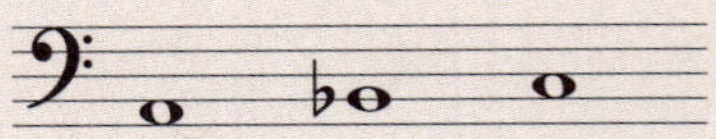

Eighth Note & Eighth Rest | **Eighth Rest & Eighth Note** | **Eighth Note & Dotted Quarter Note**

ENHARMONICS **C♯** **D♭** **F♯** **G♭**

11. CHROMA-ZONE

12. BILLY BOY

American Folk Song

13. TECHNIQUE TRAX

14. SALSA SIESTA – Duet

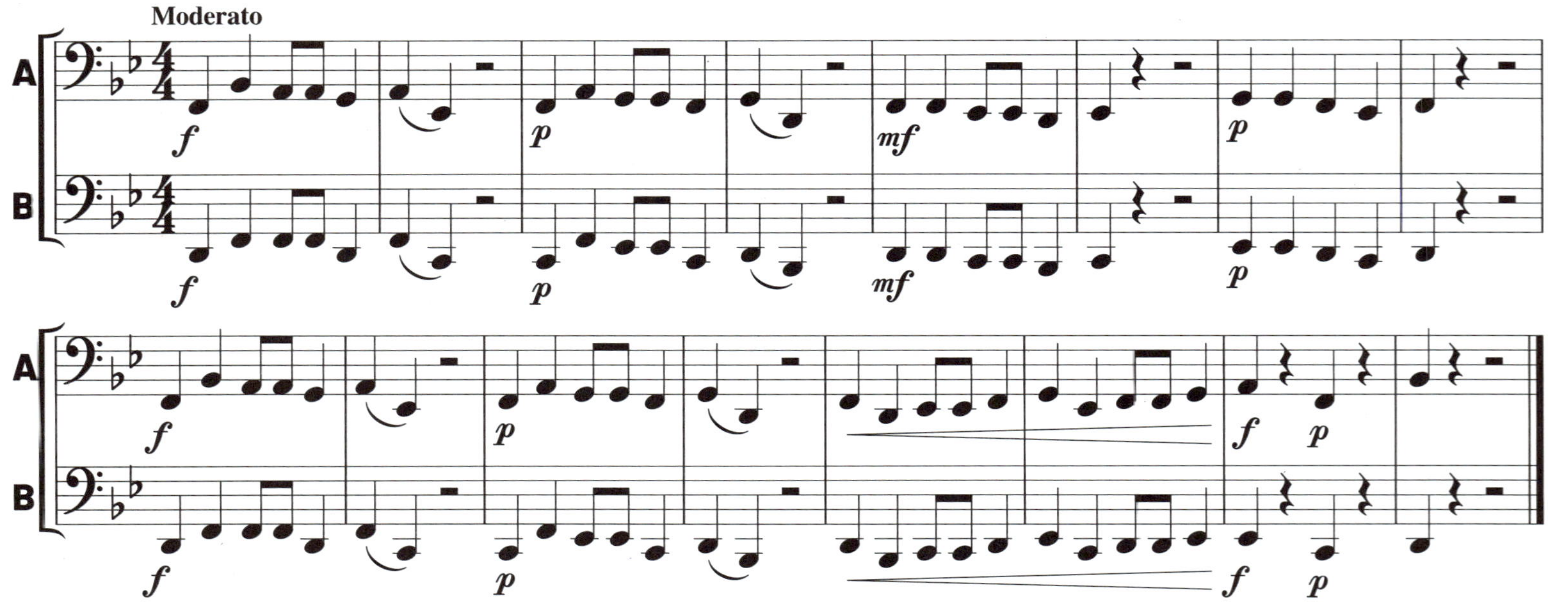

Staccato

Staccato notes are played lightly and with separation.
They are marked with a dot above or below the note.

15. TREADING LIGHTLY

Moderato

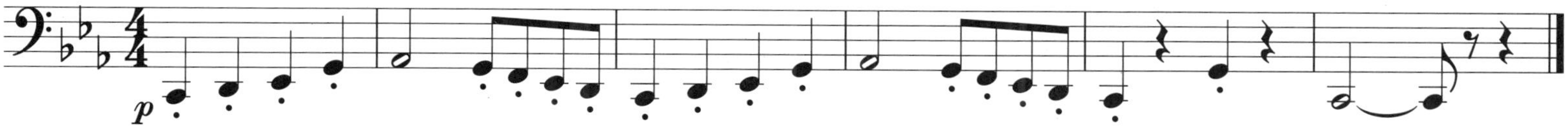

Tenuto

Tenuto notes are played smoothly and connected, holding each note until the next is played. They are marked with a straight line above or below the note.

16. SMOOTH MOVE

Moderato

17. SHIFTING GEARS

Moderato

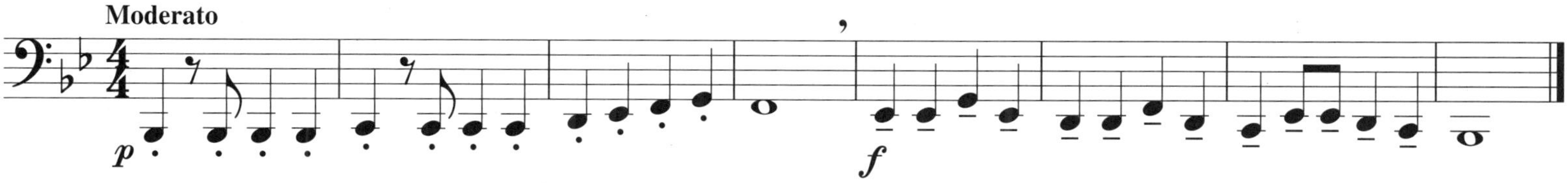

HISTORY

English composer **Thomas Tallis** (1508–1585) served as a royal court composer for Kings Henry VIII and Edward VI, and Queens Mary and Elizabeth. During Tallis' lifetime, the artist Michelangelo painted the Sistine Chapel.

Canons (one or more parts imitating the first part) were used in many forms by 16th century composers. A **Round** is a strict (or exact) canon which can be repeated any number of times without stopping. Play *Tallis Canon* as a 4-part round.

18. TALLIS CANON (Round)

Thomas Tallis

Moderato

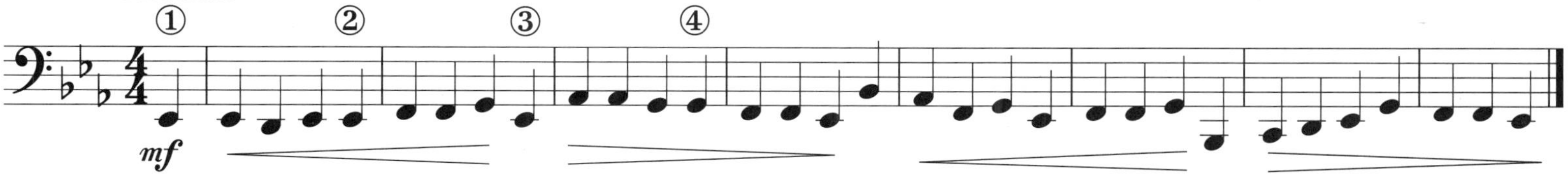

Sightreading

Sightreading means playing a musical piece for the first time. The key to sightreading success is to know what to look for *before* you play. Use the word **S-T-A-R-S** to remind yourself what to look for, and eventually your band will become sightreading STARS!

- **S** – **Sharps or flats** in the key signature
- **T** – **Time signature** and **tempo markings**
- **A** – **Accidentals** not found in the key signature
- **R** – **Rhythms**, silently counting the more difficult notes and rests
- **S** – **Signs**, including dynamics, articulations, repeats and endings

19. SIGHTREADING CHALLENGE

Moderato

DAILY WARM-UPS

WORK-OUTS FOR TONE & TECHNIQUE

20. TONE BUILDER

21. FLEXIBILITY STUDY

22. TECHNIQUE TRAX

23. CHORALE

Johann Sebastian Bach

Andante

24. GRANDFATHER'S CLOCK

Henry C. Work

Allegro

Ritardando *ritard.* (or) *rit.* – Gradually slower.

25. GLOW WORM

Paul Lincke

Allegretto ◄ *Usually a little slower than Allegro, and with a lighter style.*

rit. ◄ *Watch your director.*

26. ALMA MATER – New Note *Practice long tones on all new notes.*

A.C. Weekes, W.M. Smith, H.S. Thompson

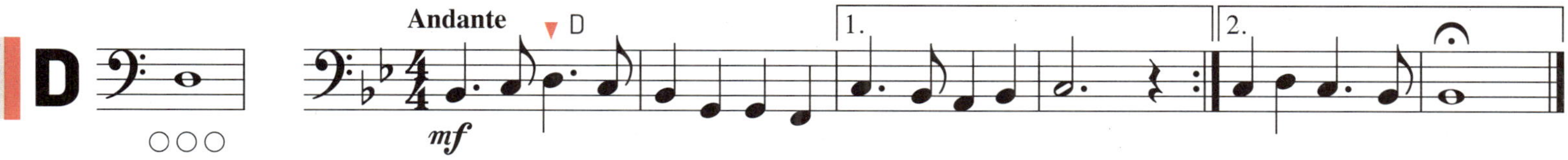

> The Scottish folk song *Loch Lomond* is credited to an anonymous soldier who was imprisoned and awaiting execution. In it he writes of his desire to return home to his family and the breathtaking beauty of Loch (Lake) Lomond, a lake in Scotland. Located in the southern highlands, the lake is almost entirely surrounded by hills. One of these is Ben Lomond, a peak 3,192 feet high.
>
> **HISTORY**

27. LOCH LOMOND

Scottish Folk Song

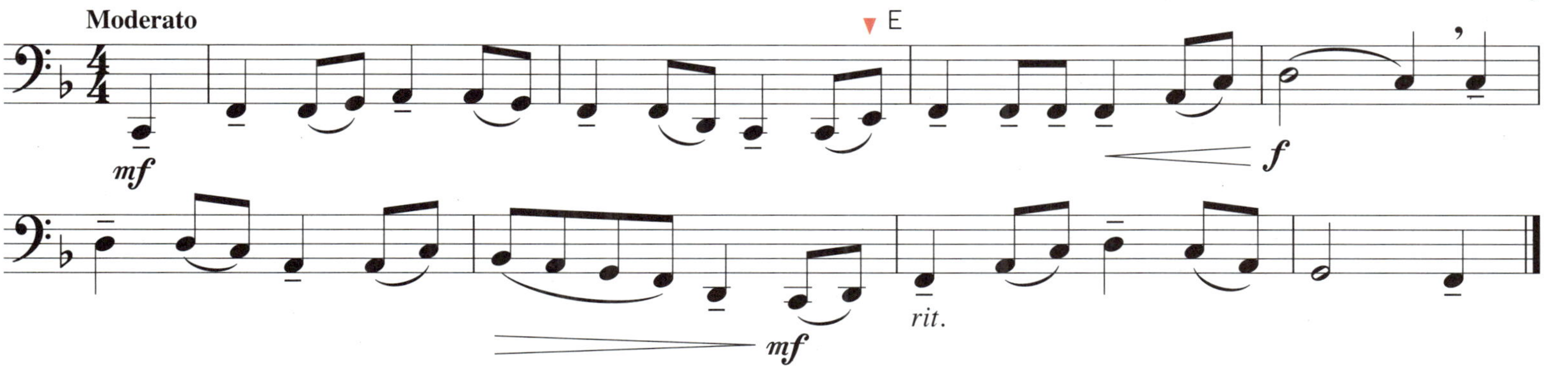

> **Key Changes**
>
> If a key signature changes during a piece of music, you will usually see a thin double bar line at the **key change**. You may also see natural signs reminding you to "cancel" previous sharps or flats. Keep playing, using the correct notes indicated in the *new* key signature.
>
> **THEORY**

28. MOLLY MALONE

Irish Folk Song

> **Dynamics**
>
> *cresc.* = *crescendo* (or)
> *decresc.* = *decrescendo* (or)

29. RISE AND FALL

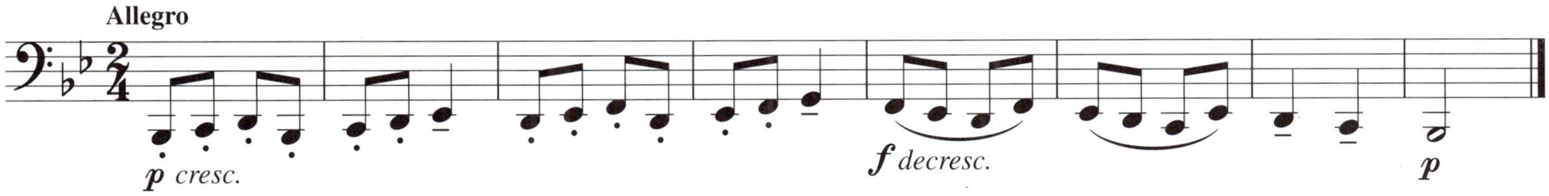

30. NO COMPARISON

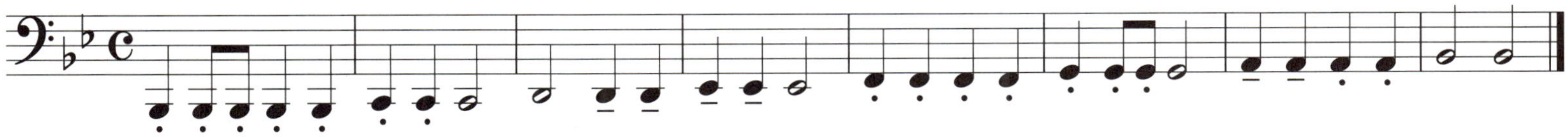

31. SIGHTREADING CHALLENGE *Remember the S-T-A-R-S guidelines.*

THEORY

₵ Time Signature
Cut Time (Alla Breve)

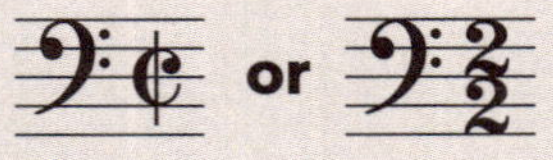

= **2 beats** per measure
= **Half** note gets one beat

𝅝 = 2 beats
𝅗𝅥 = 1 beat
♩ = ½ beat

32. RHYTHM RAP *Clap the rhythm while counting and tapping.*

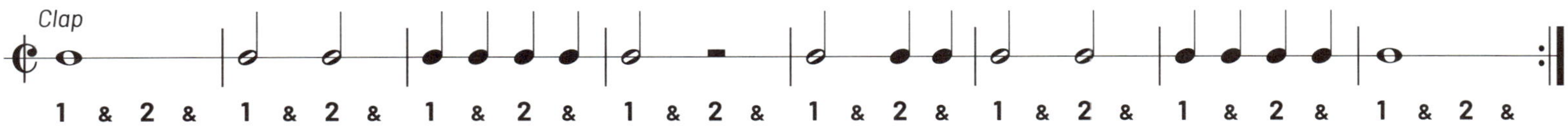

33. A CUT ABOVE

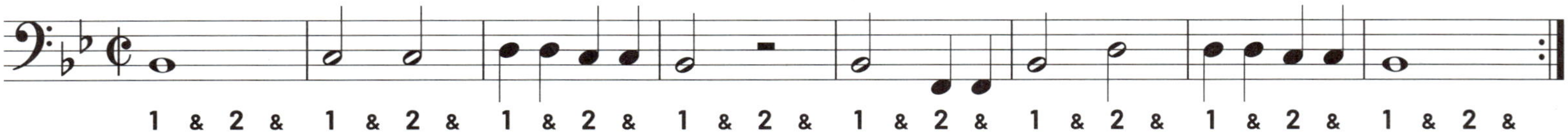

34. TWO-FOUR YANKEE DOODLE
American Folk Song

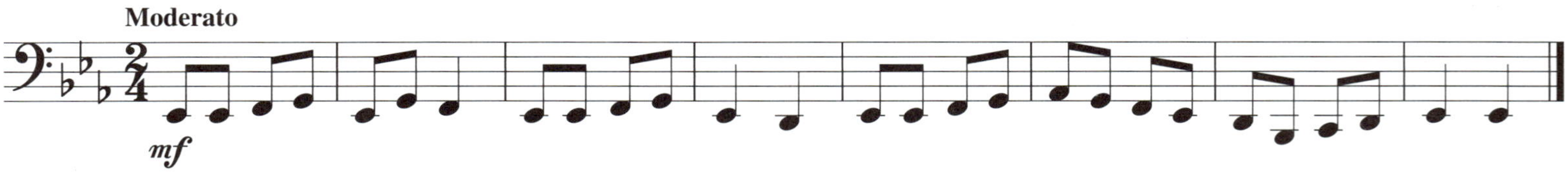

35. CUT TIME YANKEE DOODLE
American Folk Song

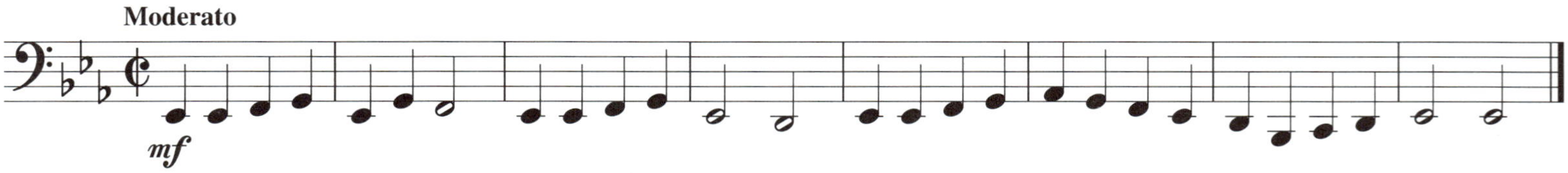

36. MARIANNE
Jamaican Folk Song

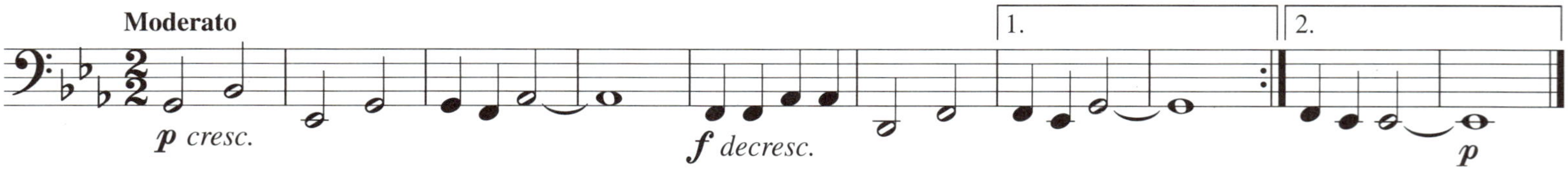

37. THE VICTORS
Louis Elbel

38. ESSENTIAL CREATIVITY *Write this example in cut time ₵ before playing.*

Dynamics

mp – *mezzo piano* (moderately soft)

Use full breath support at all dynamic levels.
p – *mp* – *mf* – *f*

39. A - ROVING

Syncopation

Syncopation occurs when an accent or emphasis is given to a note that is not on a strong beat. This type of "off-beat" feel is common in many popular and classical styles.

THEORY

40. RHYTHM RAP

41. IN SYNC

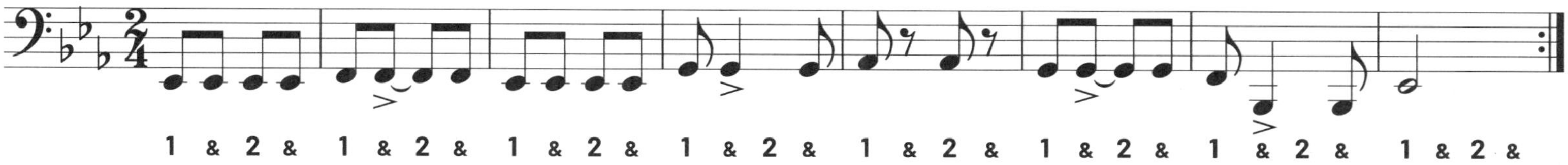

42. LA ROCA

Puerto Rican Folk Song

American composer **George M. Cohan** (1878–1942) was also a popular author, producer, director and performer. He helped develop a popular form of American musical theater now known as musical comedy. He is also considered to be one of the most famous composers of American patriotic songs, earning the Congressional Medal of Honor in 1917 for his song *Over There*. Many of his songs became morale boosters when the United States entered World War I in that same year.

HISTORY

43. ESSENTIAL ELEMENTS QUIZ – YOU'RE A GRAND OLD FLAG

Words and Music by George M. Cohan

THEORY

New Key Signature

This key signature indicates your **Key of C** (no flats or sharps).

44. KEY MOMENT – New Note

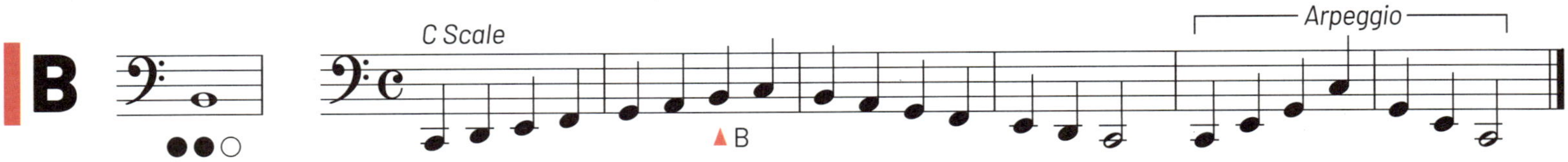

45. THE MINSTREL BOY

Irish Folk Song

46. CLOSE CALL – New Note

47. VICTORY MARCH

M. J. Shea

THEORY

Cut Time Syncopation

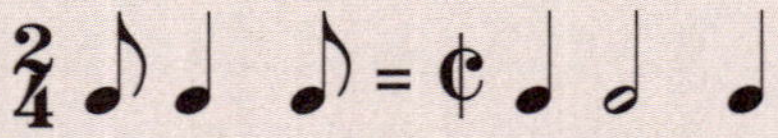

Compare the notation of the melody below with *Victory March* above. Should they sound the same?

48. WINNING STREAK

See inside front cover for information on accessing instructional videos.

M. J. Shea

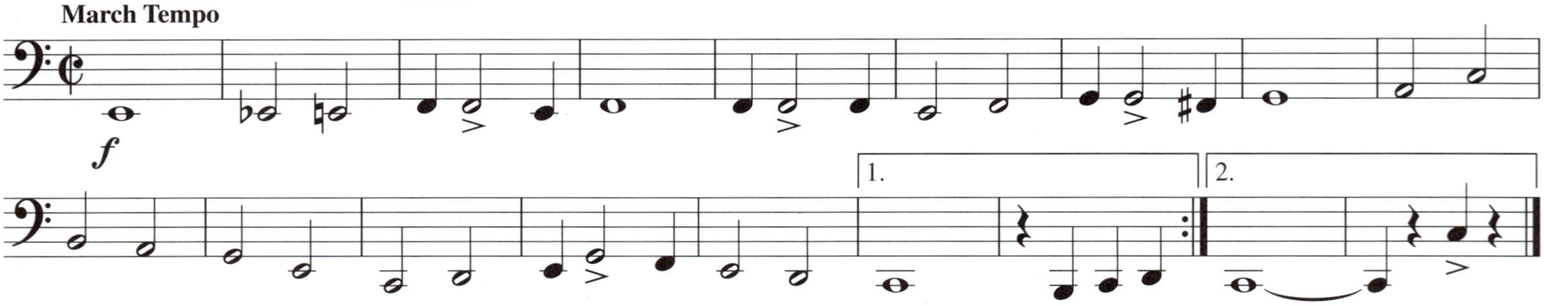

49. SIGHTREADING CHALLENGE

Remember the S-T-A-R-S guidelines.

Sixteenth Notes

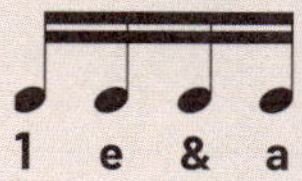

4 sixteenth notes = 1 Beat
Each sixteenth note = ¼ Beat

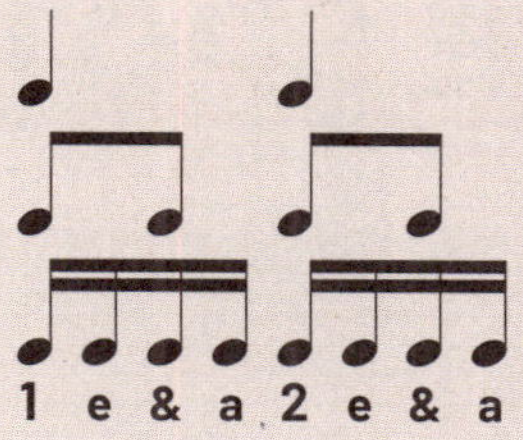

A single sixteenth note has 2 flags on the stem.

50. RHYTHM RAP

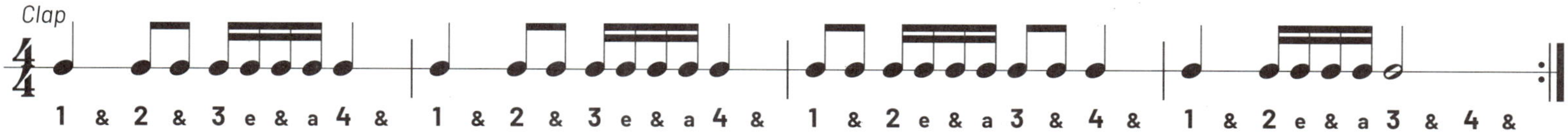

51. SIXTEENTH NOTE FANFARE

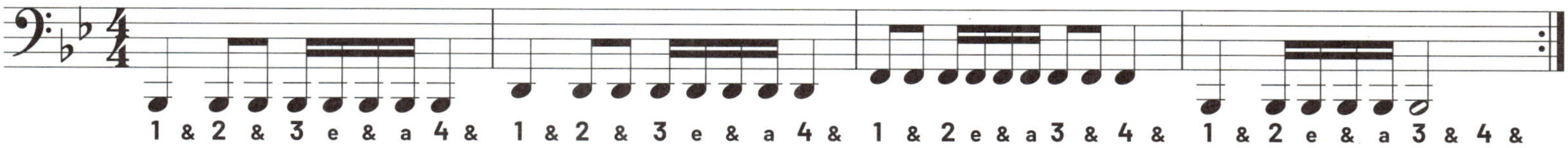

52. MOVING ALONG

53. BACK AND FORTH – Duet

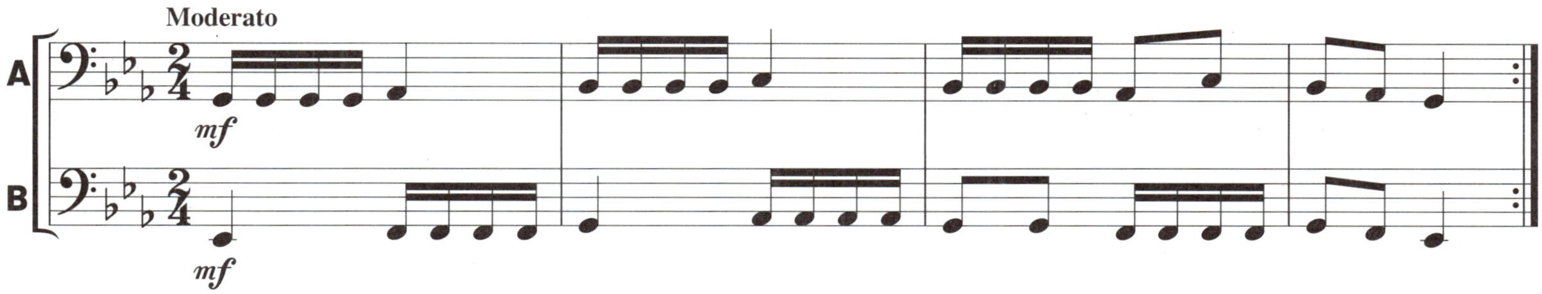

54. COMIN' ROUND THE MOUNTAIN VARIATIONS

American Folk Song

55. ESSENTIAL ELEMENTS QUIZ

PERFORMANCE SPOTLIGHT

56. WARM-UP CHORALE

J. S. Bach/Arr. by John Higgins

57. THE THUNDERER – Band Arrangement

John Philip Sousa
Arr. by John Higgins

58. HILL AND GULLY RIDER – Band Arrangement

Jamaican Folk Song
Arr. by John Higgins

59. SHENANDOAH – Band Arrangement

American Folk Song
Arr. by John Higgins

PERFORMANCE SPOTLIGHT

60. LAS MAÑANITAS – Band Arrangement

Mexican Folk Song
Arr. by John Higgins

61. RONDEAU – Band Arrangement

Jean-Joseph Mouret
Arr. by John Higgins

62. ROCK.COM – Encore Band Arrangement

John Higgins

63. RHYTHM RAP

64. SIXTEENTH VARIATIONS

65. SEA CHANTEY

66. AMERICAN FANFARE – New Note

THEORY

New Key Signature

This key signature indicates your **Key of A♭**. Play all B's as B-flat, all E's as E-flat, all A's as A-flat, and all D's as D-flat.

67. SCALE STUDY

68. BILL BAILEY

Hughie Cannon

69. RHYTHM RAP

70. RHYTHM ETUDE

71. BATTLE STATIONS

72. ENGLISH DANCE

73. BIG ROCK CANDY MOUNTAIN

American Folk Song

74. ESSENTIAL ELEMENTS QUIZ

Looking for some more fun music to play?
See the inside front cover for instructions on accessing recent popular Bonus Songs.

Rallentando *rall.* – Gradually slower (same as *ritardando*).

75. SIMPLE SONG – Duet

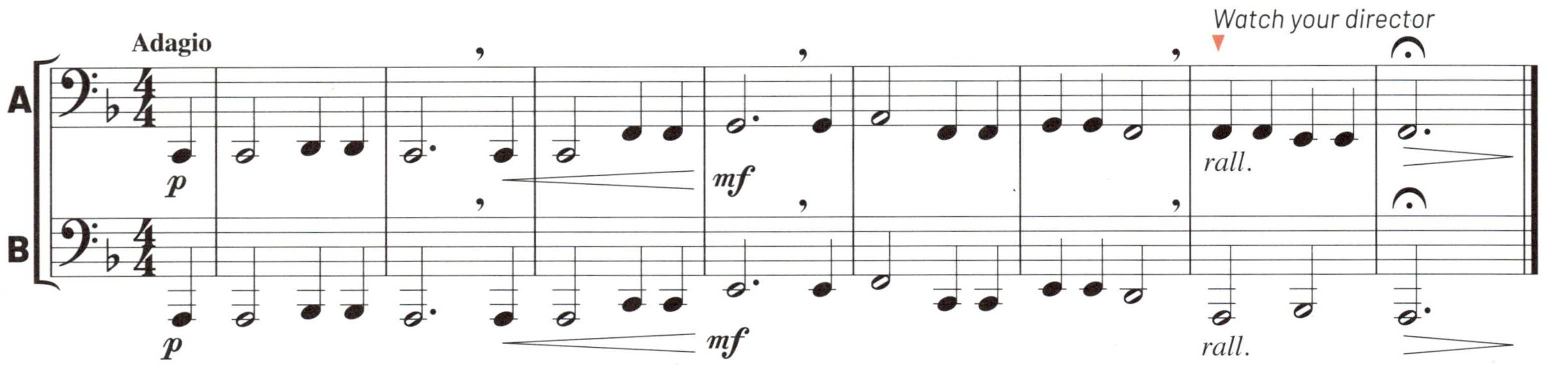

76. LINE DANCE

77. TECHNIQUE TRAX

78. THE GALWAY PIPER

Irish Reel

79. MANHATTAN BEACH MARCH

John Philip Sousa

80. SIGHTREADING CHALLENGE *Remember the S-T-A-R-S guidelines.*

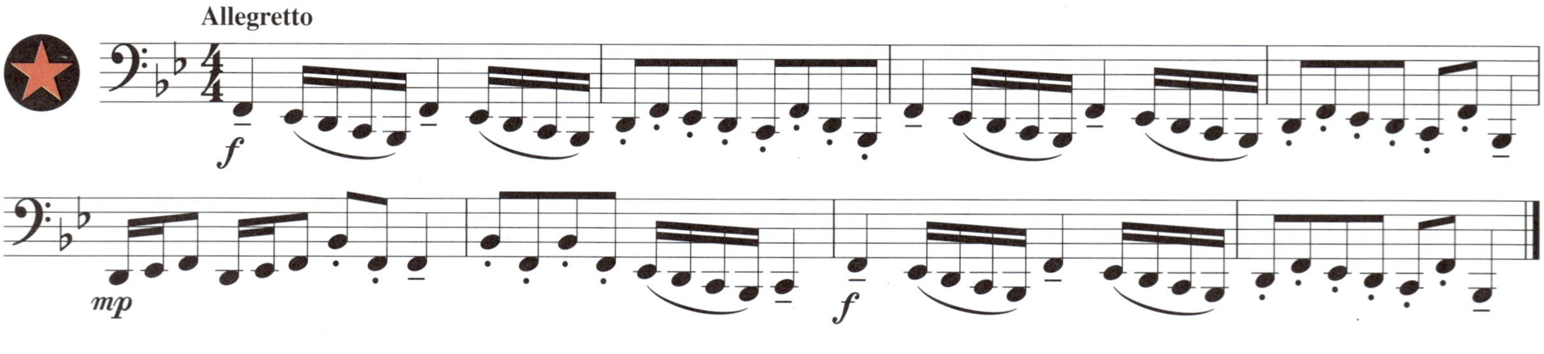

81. RHYTHM RAP

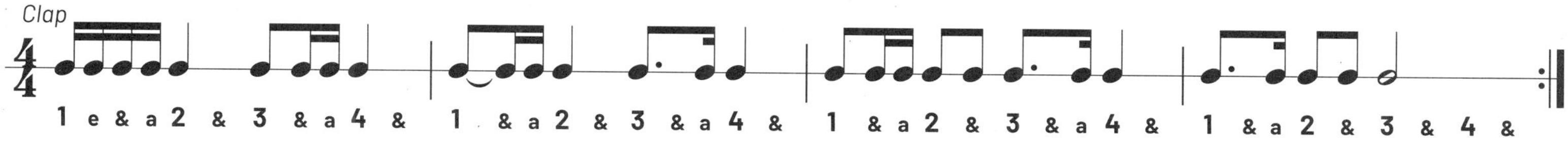

82. MARCHING ALONG

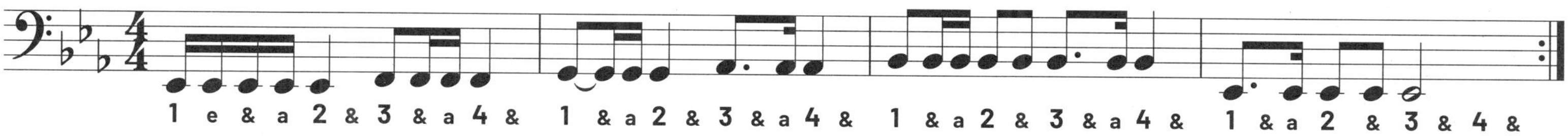

83. FANFARE FOR BAND – Trio

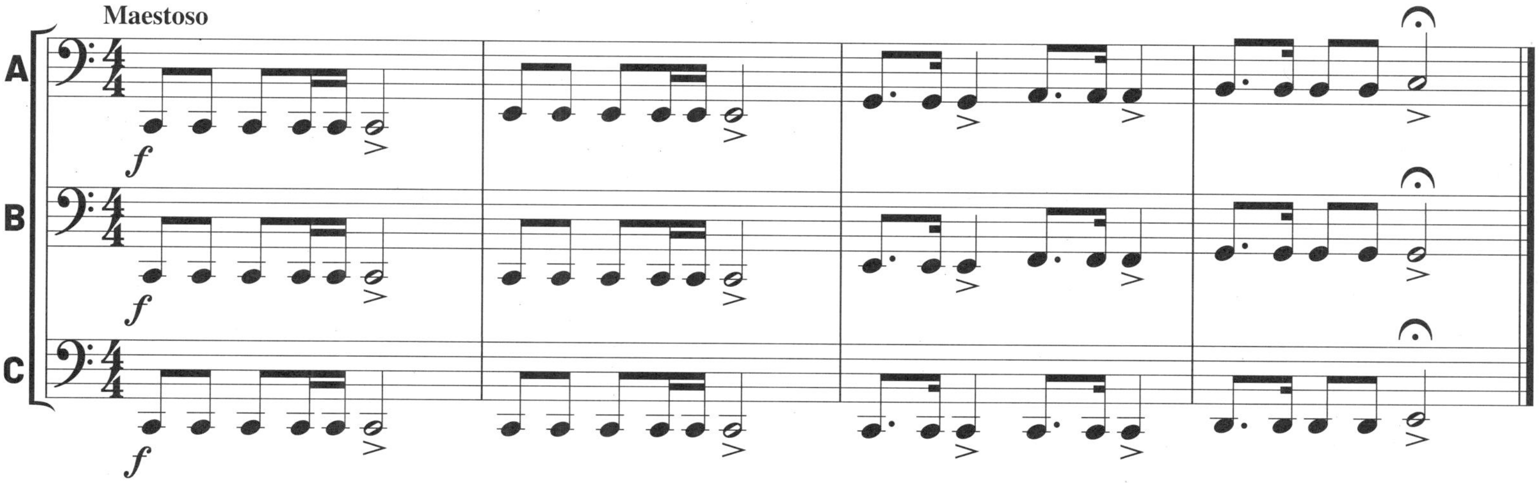

84. O TANNENBAUM

German Carol

85. S'VIVON

Traditional Hanukkah Song

86. GOOD KING WENCESLAS

English Carol

DAILY WARM-UPS

WORK-OUTS FOR TONE & TECHNIQUE

87. TONE BUILDER

Play at a very slow tempo.

88. FLEXIBILITY STUDY

89. TECHNIQUE TRAX

90. CHORALE

Johann Sebastian Bach

HISTORY

French composer **Georges Bizet** (1838–1875) entered the Paris Conservatory to study music when he was only ten years old. There he won many awards for voice, piano, organ, and composition. Bizet's best known composition is the opera *Carmen*, which was first performed in 1875. *Carmen* tells the story of a band of Gypsies, soldiers, smugglers, and outlaws. Originally criticized for its realism on stage, it was soon hailed as the most popular French opera ever written.

91. TOREADOR SONG (from CARMEN)

Georges Bizet

92. LA CUMPARSITA

G. Rodriguez

93. THE YELLOW ROSE OF TEXAS

Check the key signature.

American Folk Song

94. SCALE STUDY – New Note

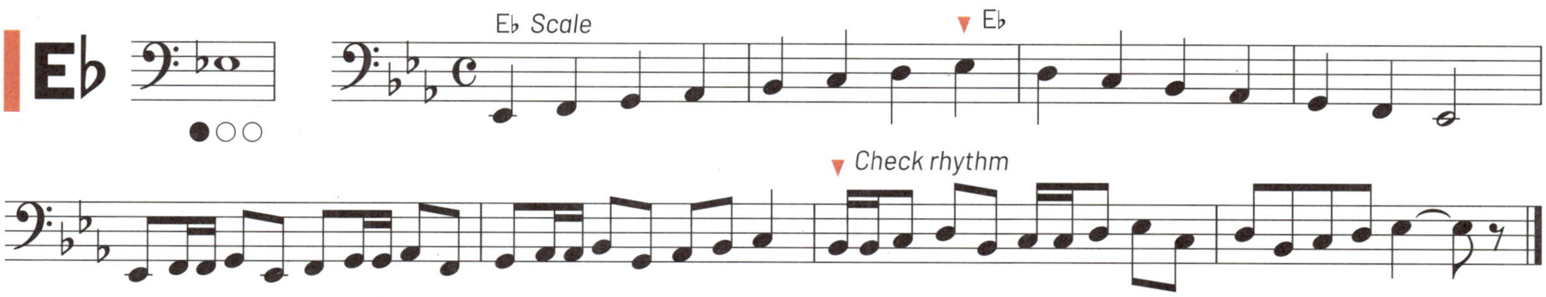

> **HISTORY**
>
> Until 1974 Australia's official national anthem was *God Save The Queen*. A competition was held in 1973 to compose a new anthem, but none of the entries met with the judges' approval. Finally the government asked the public to vote, choosing from among Australia's 3 most popular patriotic songs. After easily defeating *Waltzing Matilda* and *God Save The Queen*, *Advance Australia Fair* was officially declared the national anthem of Australia on April 19, 1974.

95. ADVANCE AUSTRALIA FAIR

Peter Dodds McCormick

96. ESSENTIAL CREATIVITY

Arrange the melody of "America (My Country 'Tis Of Thee)" for your instrument. Write out the first line (6 measures). Your first note is F. ADD: Key signature—key of F • Time signature—3/4 • Tempo and dynamic markings.

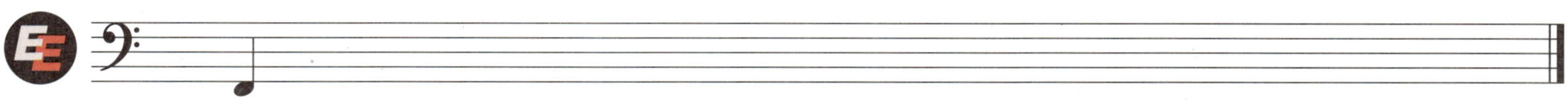

Play the completed line on your instrument to hear your own version.

97. AMERICAN PATROL

F. W. Meacham

98. ARIA (from MARRIAGE OF FIGARO)

Wolfgang Amadeus Mozart

HISTORY

American composer **John Philip Sousa** (1854–1932) was best known for his brilliant band marches. Sousa wrote 136 marches, including *The Stars and Stripes Forever*, which was declared the official march of the United States of America in 1987.

99. THE STARS AND STRIPES FOREVER

John Philip Sousa

100. SIGHTREADING CHALLENGE

Remember the S-T-A-R-S guidelines.

6/8 Time Signature

6/8 = **6 beats** per measure
= **Eighth** note gets one beat

♪ = 1 beat   ♩ = 2 beats
♩. = 3 beats   𝅗𝅥. = 6 beats

THEORY

6/8 time is usually played with a slight emphasis on the **1st** and **4th** beats of each measure. This divides the measure into 2 groups of 3 beats each. In faster music, these two primary beats will make the music feel like it's counted "in 2."

101. RHYTHM RAP *Clap the rhythm while counting and tapping.*

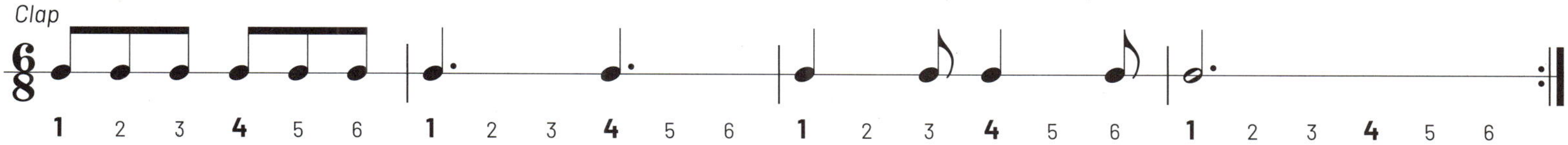

102. LAZY DAY

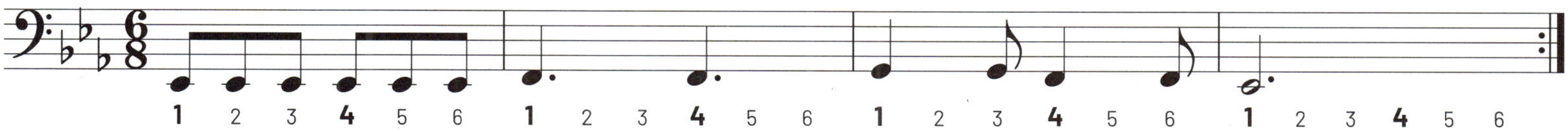

103. ROW YOUR BOAT

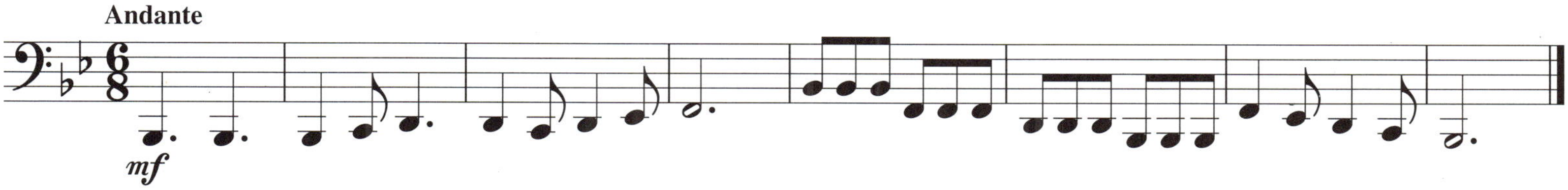

104. JOLLY GOOD FELLOW

105. CHANSON

French Folk Song

106. ESSENTIAL ELEMENTS QUIZ – WHEN JOHNNY COMES MARCHING HOME

American Folk Song

THEORY

More Enharmonics

Remember that notes which sound the same but have different letter names are called **enharmonics**. These are some common enharmonics that you'll use in the exercises below.

More Chromatics

The smallest distance between two notes is a half-step, and a scale made up of consecutive half-steps is a **chromatic scale**. These are usually written with **enharmonic** notes—sharps when going up and flats when going down.

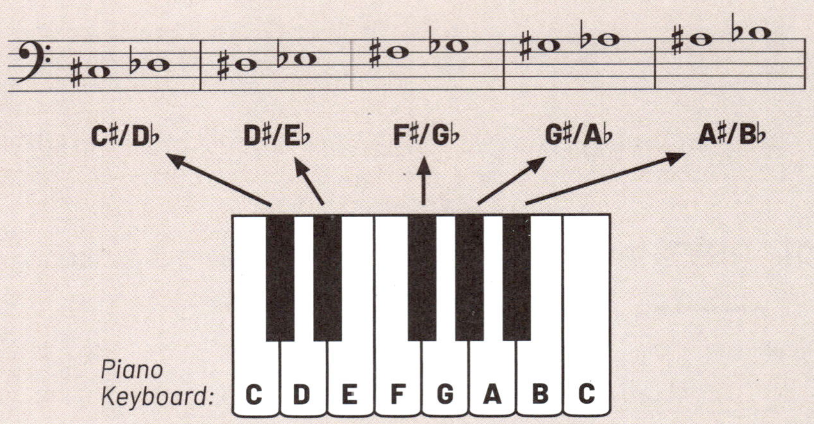

107. CHROMATIC SCALE *Practice slowly until you are sure of all the fingerings.*

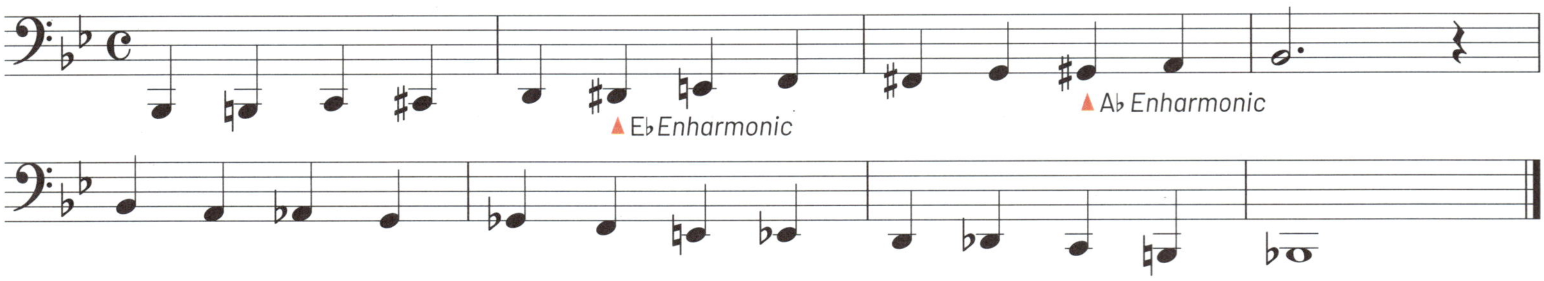

108. TECHNIQUE TRAX

HISTORY

A **Habañera** is a Cuban dance and song form in slow 2/4 meter. It is named after the city of Havana, the capital of Cuba. Made popular in the New World in the early 19th Century, it was later carried over to Spain. There the rhythms of the Habañera were incorporated into many styles of Latin music. One of the most famous Habañeras is heard in Bizet's *Carmen*, written in 1875.

109. HABAÑERA (from CARMEN)

Georges Bizet

Andante

110. CHROMATIC CRESCENDO

Moderato

111. TURKISH MARCH (from THE RUINS OF ATHENS)

Ludwig van Beethoven

112. THE OVERLANDER

Australian Folk Song

113. STACCATO STUDY

114. YANKEE DOODLE DANDY

Words and Music by George M. Cohan

115. SIGHTREADING CHALLENGE

Remember the **S-T-A-R-S** guidelines:
S – Sharps or flats in the key signature, **T** – Time signature and tempos, **A** – Accidentals, **R** – Rhythm, **S** – Signs

THEORY

Triplets

A **triplet** is a group of **3** notes played in the space of **2**. In $\frac{2}{4}$, $\frac{3}{4}$, or $\frac{4}{4}$ time, an eighth note triplet is spread evenly across one beat.

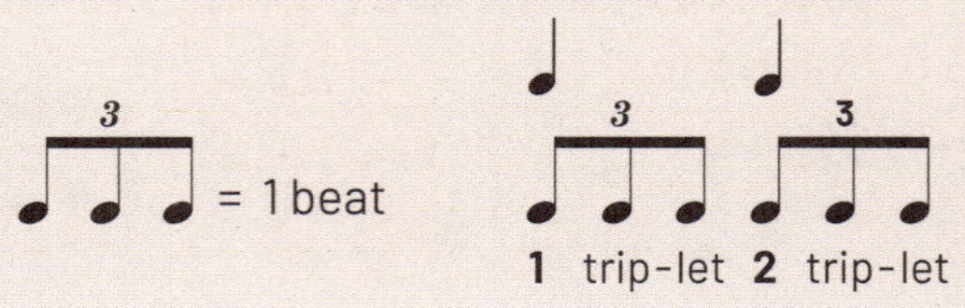

116. RHYTHM RAP

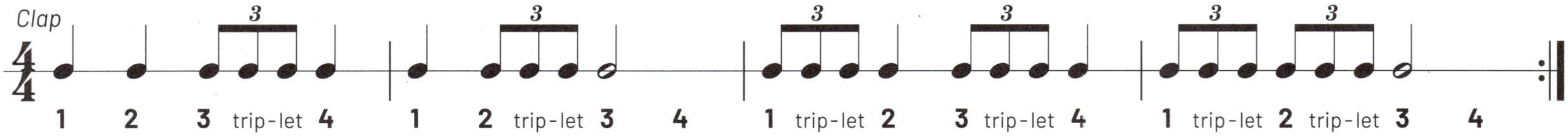

117. THREE TO GET READY

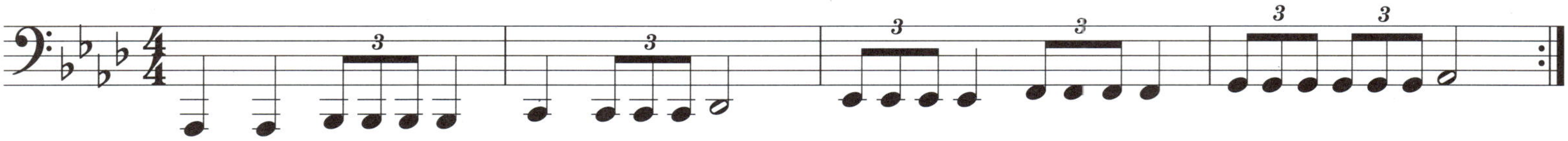

118. TRIPLET STUDY

119. MARCH (from THE NUTCRACKER) – Duet

Peter I. Tchaikovsky

120. ESSENTIAL ELEMENTS QUIZ – THEME FROM FAUST

Charles Gounod

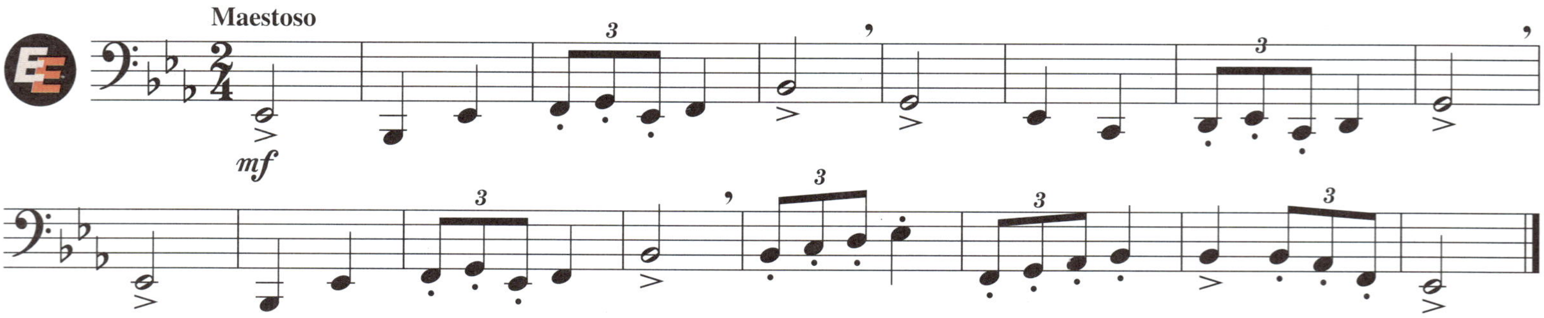

121. SCALE STUDY – New Notes

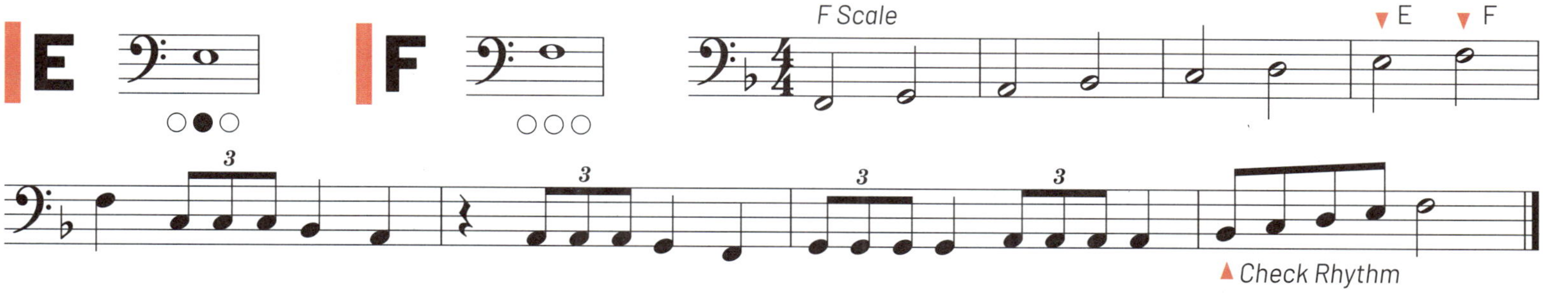

122. OVER THE RIVER AND THROUGH THE WOODS

American Folk Song

123. RHYTHM RAP

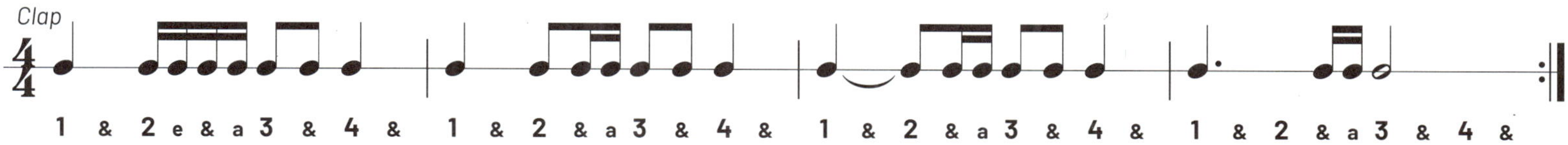

124. ON THE MOVE

125. HIGHER GROUND

126. ESSENTIAL ELEMENTS QUIZ

HISTORY

The first known printing of the lyrics and music to **The Marines' Hymn** dates from August 1, 1918. An unknown author is believed to have taken the opening words of the song from the words on the Marine Corps flag, "From the halls of Montezuma to the shores of Tripoli." The music was taken from "Genevieve de Brabant," by the operetta composer Jacques Offenbach.

127. THE MARINES' HYMN

D.S. al Fine

Play until you see the **D.S. al Fine**. Then go back to the sign (𝄋) and play until the word **Fine**. **D.S.** is the abbreviation for **Dal Segno**, or "from the sign," and **Fine** means "the end."

128. D.S. MARCH

Accelerando

accel. – Gradually faster.

129. CAN-CAN

Jacques Offenbach

▲ *Watch your director.*

130. TARANTELLA

Italian Folk Song

Allegro

> The **waltz** is a dance in moderate 3/4 time which developed around 1800 from the Ländler, an Austrian peasant dance. Austrian composer **Johann Strauss, Jr.** (1825–1899) composed over 400 waltzes. These include such famous pieces as *The Blue Danube*, *Tales From the Vienna Woods* and *Emperor Waltz*.
>
> HISTORY

131. EMPEROR WALTZ

Johann Strauss, Jr.

Andantino ◄ *Tempo between Andante and Moderato.*

Legato Style

legato – Played in a smooth, connected style.

132. ENGLISH DANCE – Duet

Johann Christian Bach

Andante

133. ESSENTIAL ELEMENTS QUIZ – BRITISH GRENADIERS

Traditional

Allegretto

134. NASSAU BOUND

Bahamian Folk Song

135. UNFINISHED SYMPHONY THEME

Franz Schubert

136. RHYTHM STUDY

Measure Repeat ⁒ Repeat the previous measure once for each **Measure Repeat** sign.

137. COUNTRY GARDENS

English Folk Song

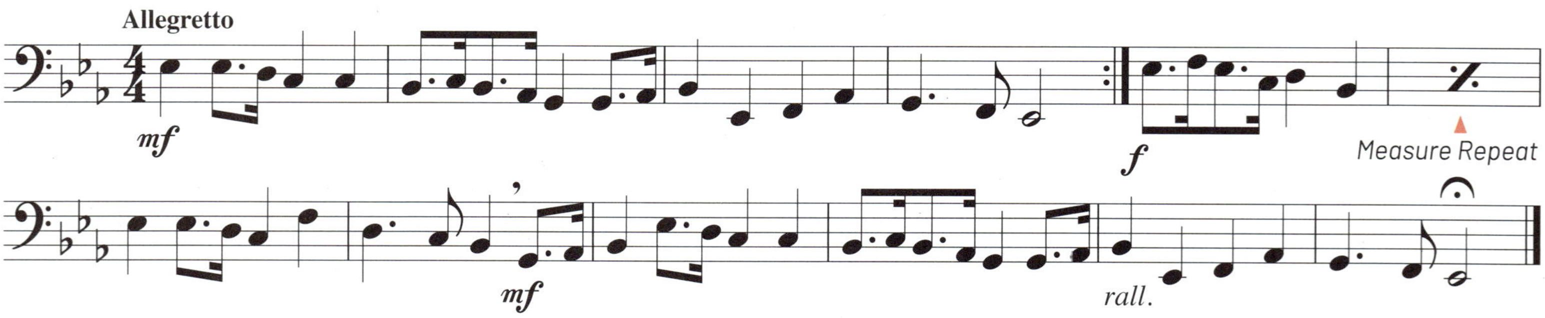

138. JOSHUA

African-American Spiritual

139. LISTEN TO THE MOCKINGBIRD

Alice Hawthorne

140. ANCHORS AWEIGH

Capt. A.H. Miles and C.A. Zimmerman

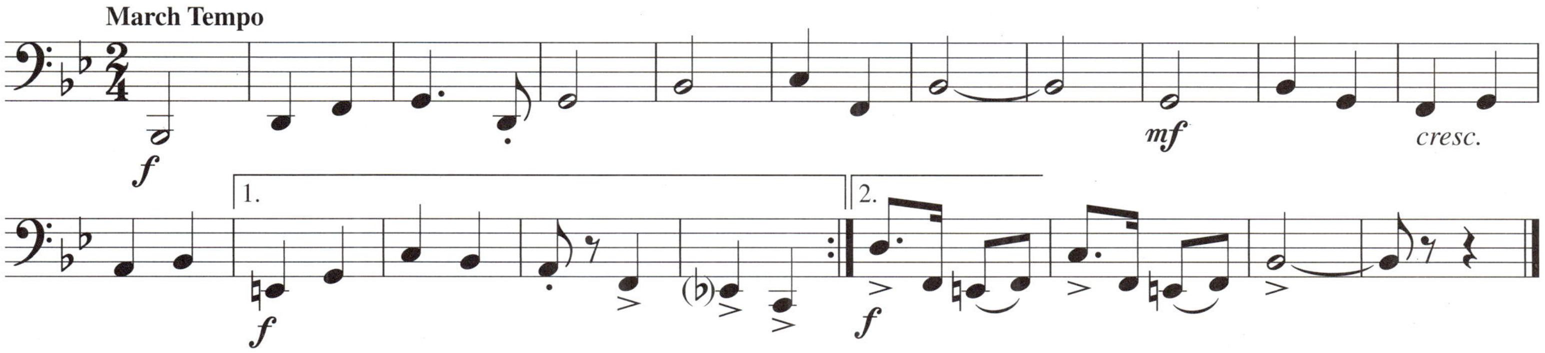

141. GREENSLEEVES

English Folk Song

142. THE LONG CLIMB

143. THE BLUE BELLS OF SCOTLAND

Scottish Folk Song

THEORY

Major and Minor

The scales you've already learned are called **Major** scales. They all follow the same pattern, with **half-steps** between notes 3-4 and between notes 7-8.

Natural Minor scales follow a different pattern, with **half-steps** between notes 2-3 and 5-6. The **G Minor** scale uses the same key signature as **B♭ Major**.

Another type of minor scale is called **Harmonic Minor**, which adds an accidental to raise the **7th** note by a half-step. Compare the scales on the right.

See page 37 for additional minor scales.

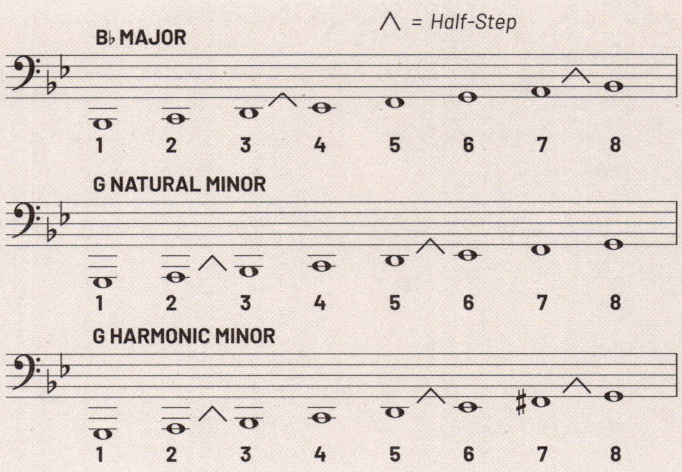

144. NATURAL MINOR SCALE – New Note

G

145. FINALE FROM "NEW WORLD SYMPHONY"

Antonin Dvorák

146. HARMONIC MINOR SCALE

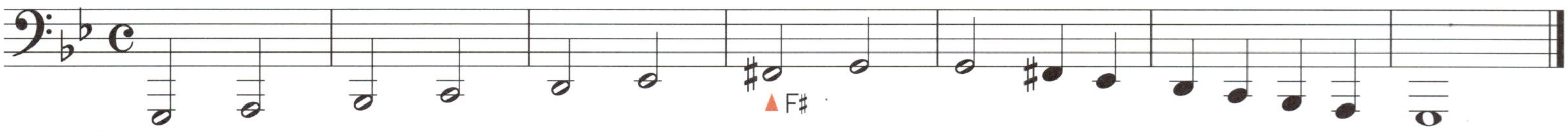

147. HUNGARIAN DANCE NO. 5

Johannes Brahms

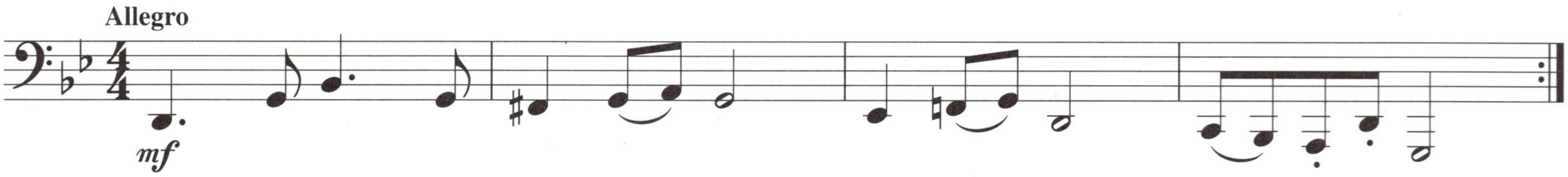

148. POMP AND CIRCUMSTANCE (LAND OF HOPE AND GLORY)

Edward Elgar

PERFORMANCE SPOTLIGHT

D.S. al Coda

Play until you see the **D.S. al Coda**. Then go back to the sign (𝄋) and play until the **Coda Sign** ("To Coda" 𝄌). Skip directly to the **Coda** and play until the end.

149. SIMPLE GIFTS – Band Arrangement

Shaker Folk Song
Arr. by John Higgins

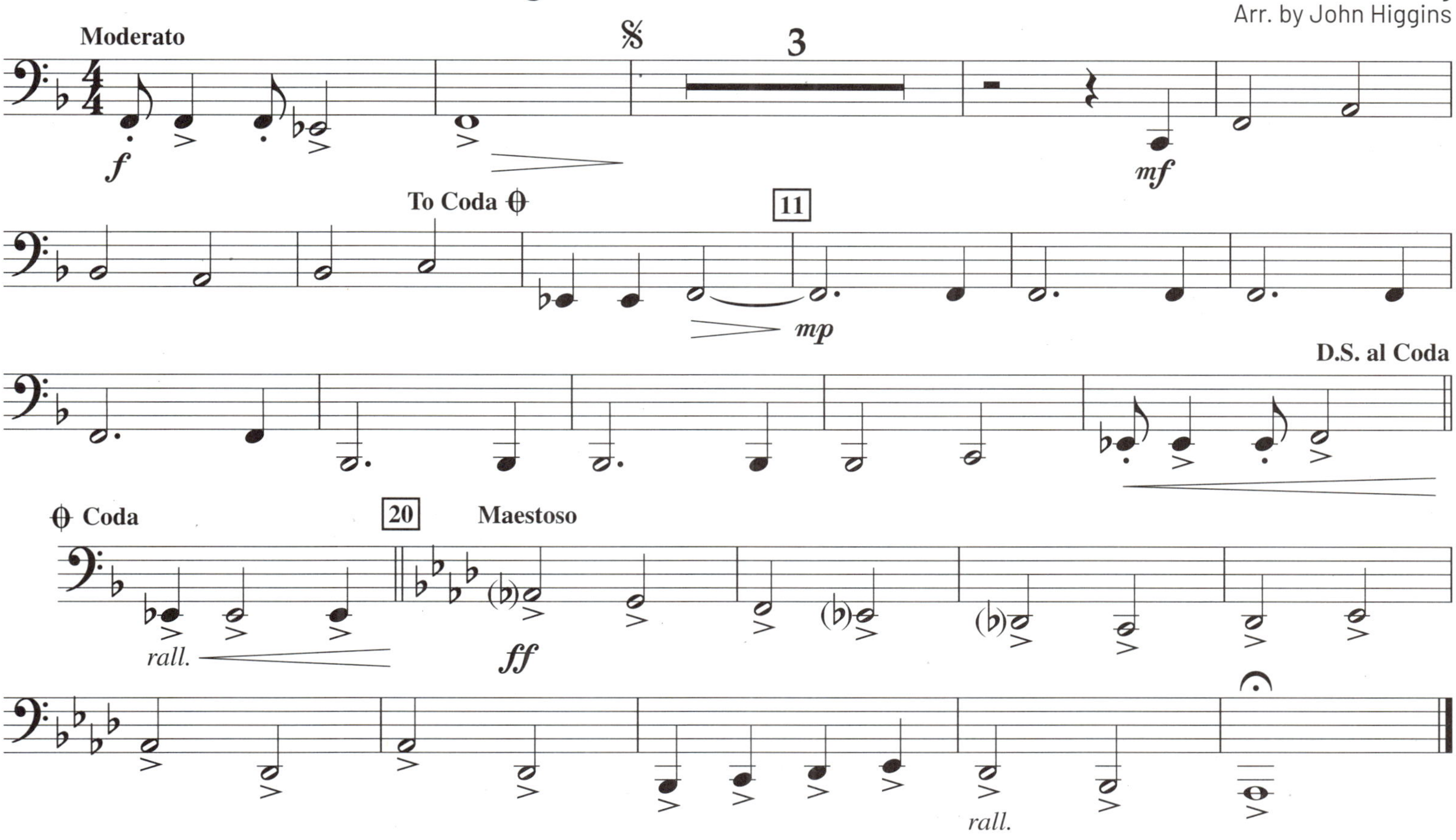

150. SEMPER FIDELIS – Band Arrangement

John Philip Sousa
Arr. by John Higgins

PERFORMANCE SPOTLIGHT

151. DANNY BOY – Band Arrangement

Irish Folk Song
Arr. by John Higgins

152. TAKE ME OUT TO THE BALL GAME – Band Arrangement

By Jack Norworth and Harry von Tilzer
Arr. by John Higgins

Additional Bonus Songs are available online. See the inside front cover for details.

PERFORMANCE SPOTLIGHT

153. SERENGETI (AFRICAN RHAPSODY) – Band Arrangement

John Higgins

RUBANK® STUDIES

154. CHORALE

155. CHORALE

156. CHORALE

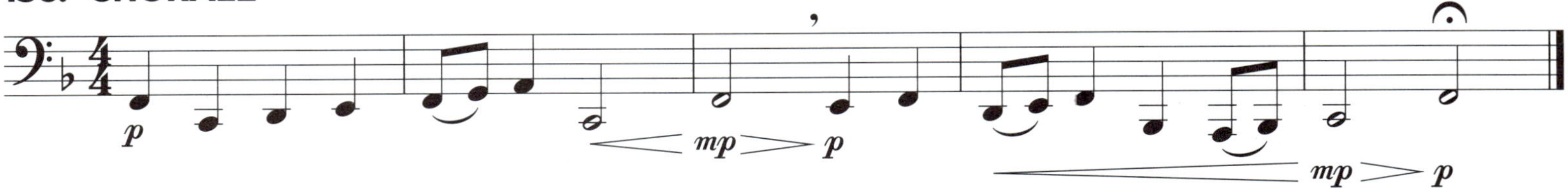

157. CHORALE

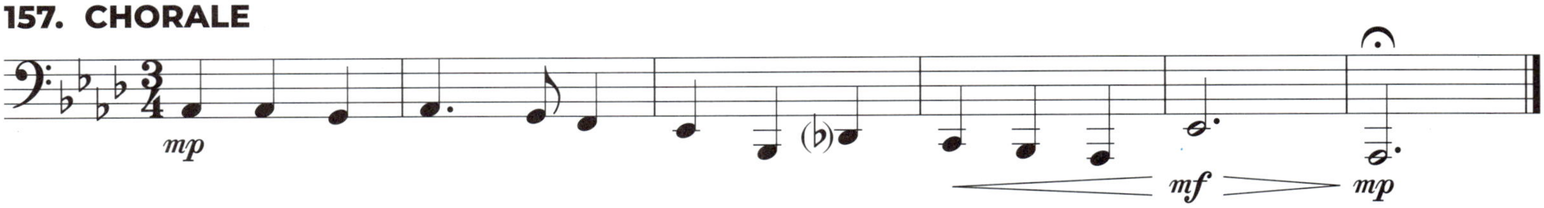

158. CHORALE

KEY OF B♭

159.

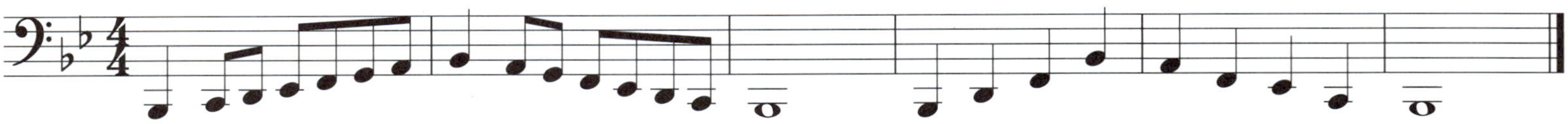

160.

161.

162.

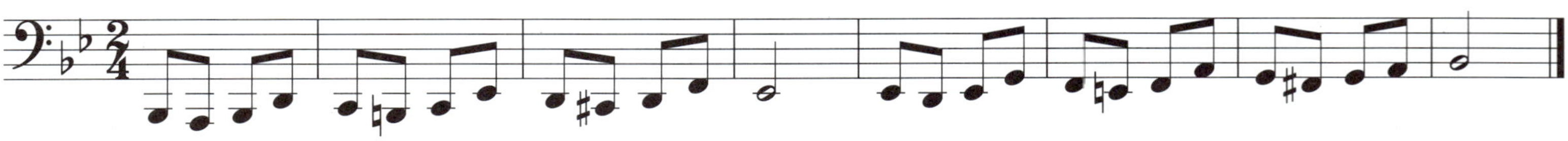

RUBANK® STUDIES

KEY OF E♭

163.

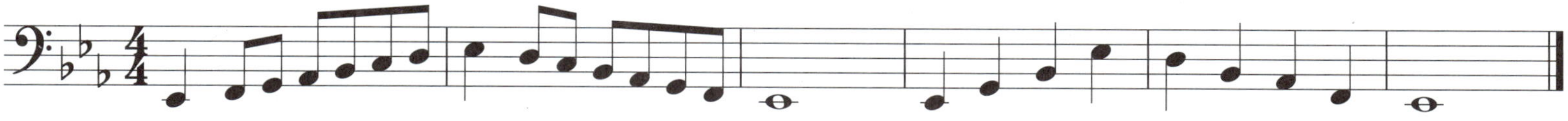

164.

165.

166.

KEY OF F

167.

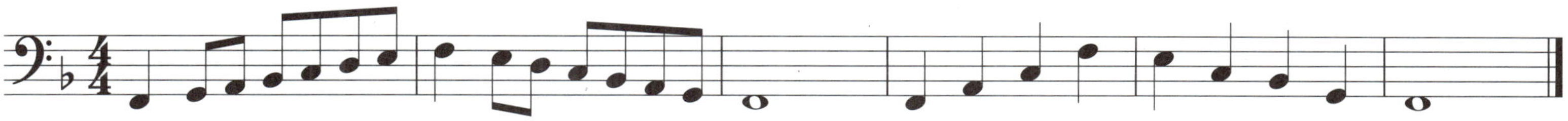

168.

169.

170.

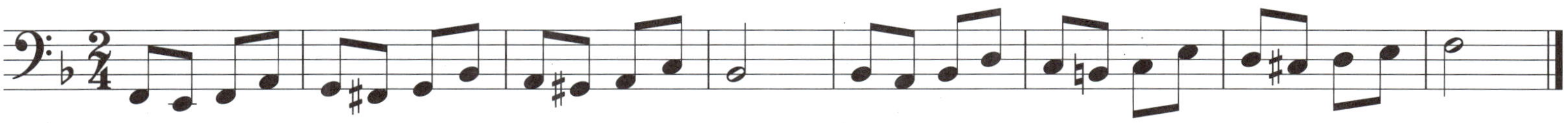

RUBANK® STUDIES

KEY OF A♭

171.

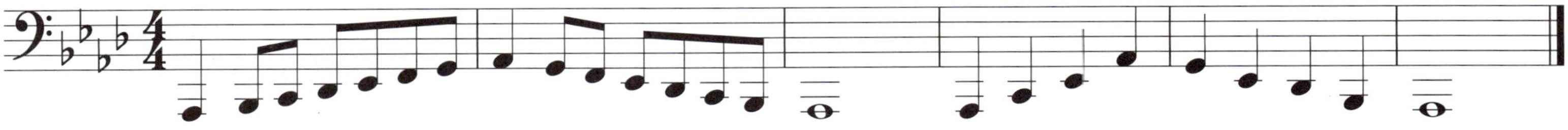

172.

173.

174.

KEY OF C

175.

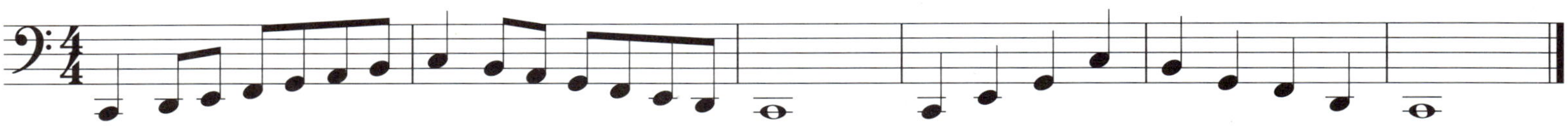

176.

177.

178.

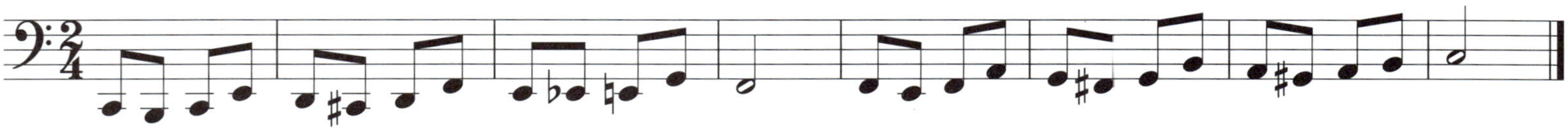

RUBANK® STUDIES

KEY OF G MINOR

179.

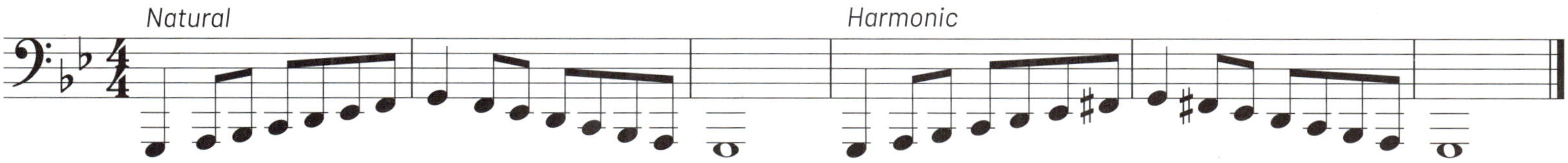

180.

KEY OF C MINOR

181.

182.

KEY OF D MINOR

183.

184.

CHROMATIC SCALES

185.

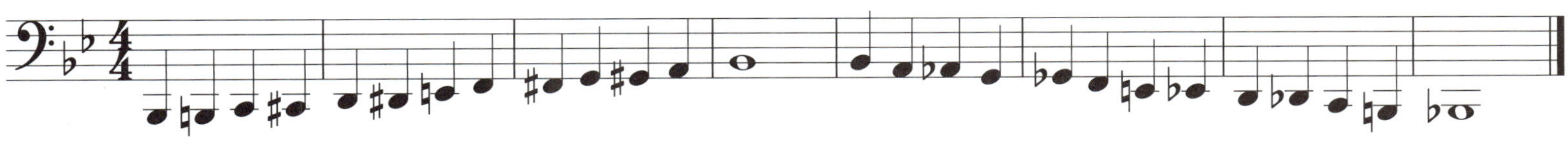

186.

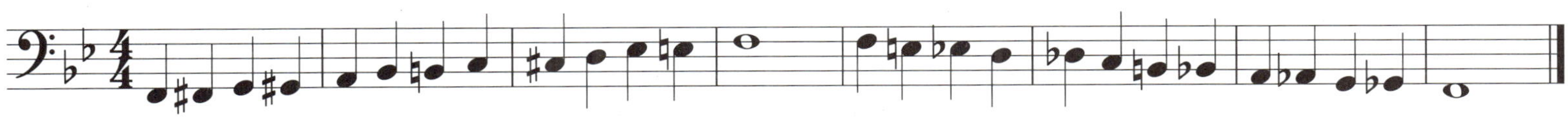

INDIVIDUAL STUDY – Tuba

187. LOW NOTE EXCURSION – New Note

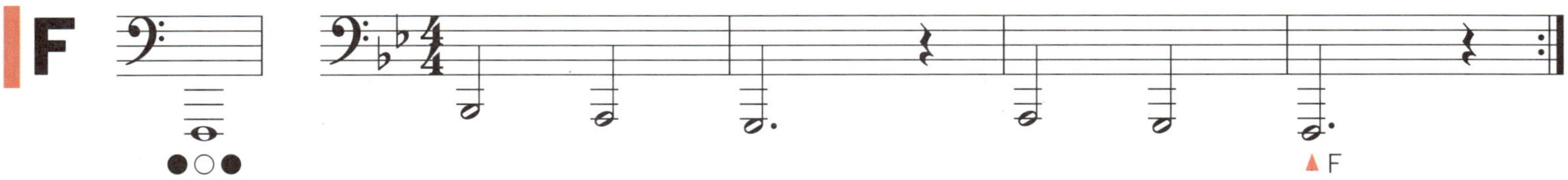

188. LOW ENHARMONIC STUDY – New Note

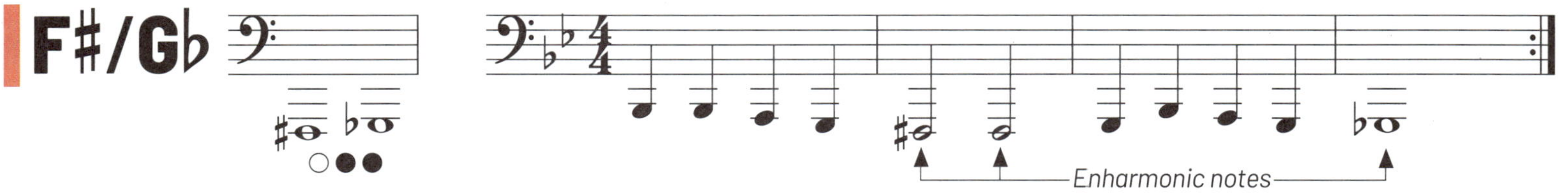

189. BREATH CONTROL EXERCISE

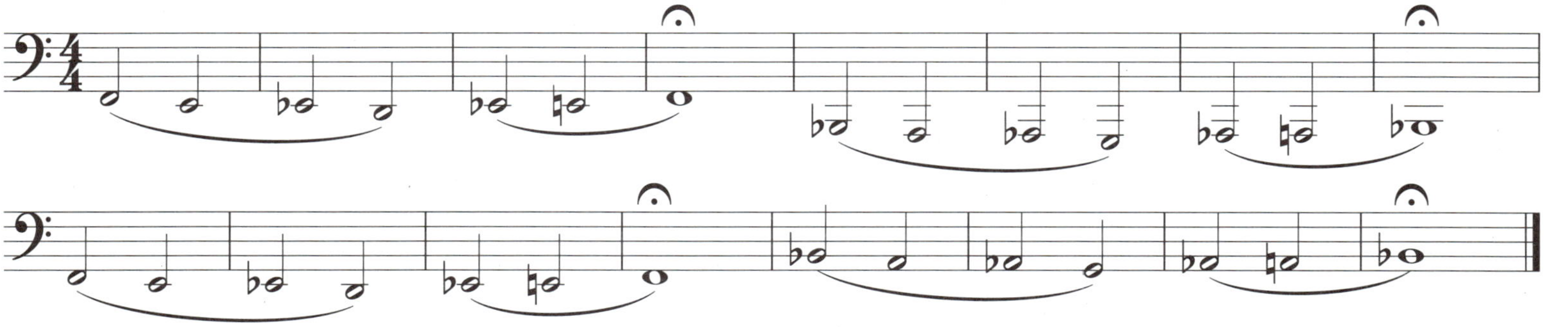

190. FLEXIBILITY STUDY #1 (Lip Slurs)

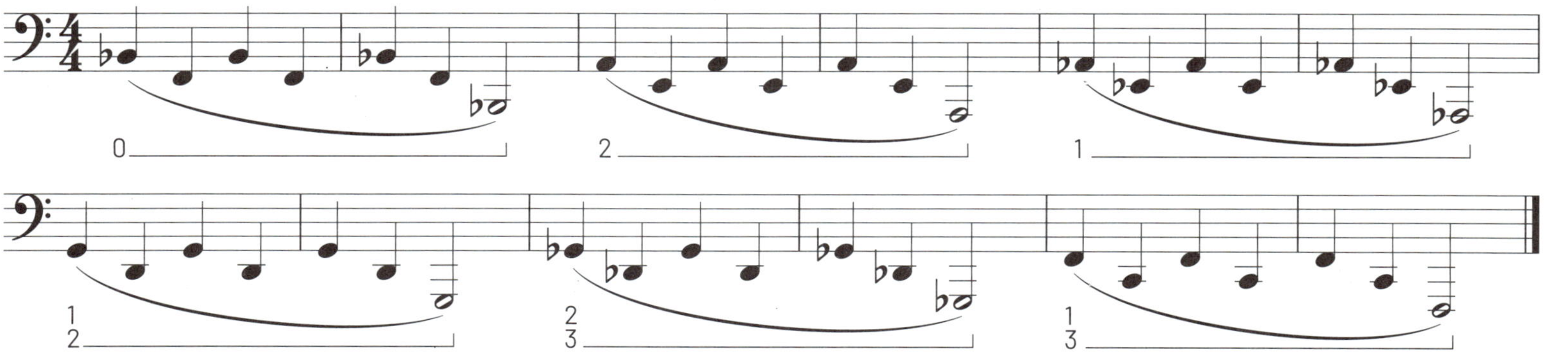

191. FLEXIBILITY STUDY #2

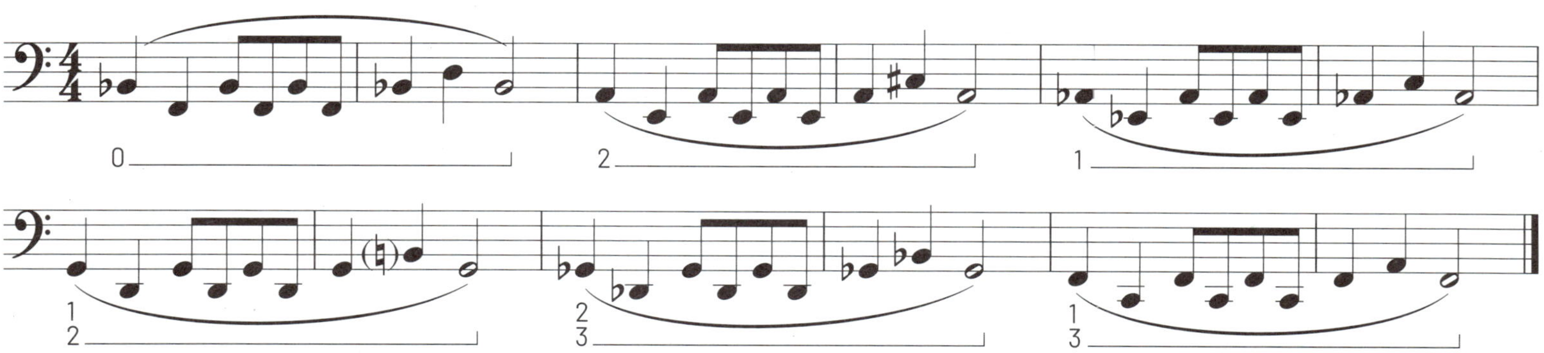

192. FINGER PATTERNS

INDIVIDUAL STUDY – Tuba

193. ARTICULATION ETUDE #1

194. ARTICULATION ETUDE #2

195. TONGUING WORK-OUT #1

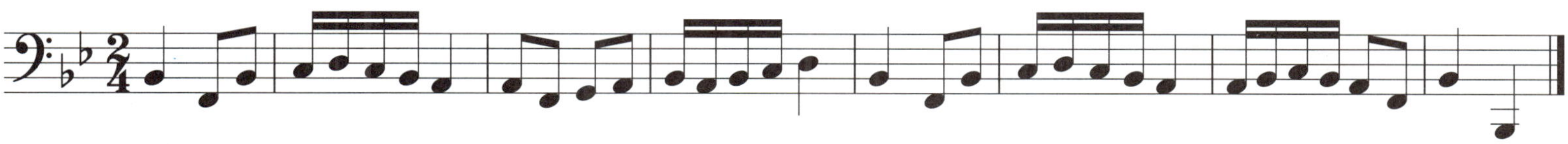

196. TONGUING WORK-OUT #2

197. TONGUING WORK-OUT #3

198. STUDY IN A♭

199. CHROMATIC CHALLENGE

INDIVIDUAL STUDY – Tuba

Solo with Piano Accompaniment

You can perform this solo with the piano accompaniment on the following page.

200. IN THE HALL OF THE MOUNTAIN KING from "Peer Gynt Suite" – Tuba Solo

Online audio – see inside front cover to access.

Edvard Grieg
Arr. by G. E. Holmes

INDIVIDUAL STUDY – Tuba

200. IN THE HALL OF THE MOUNTAIN KING from "Peer Gynt Suite" – Piano Accompaniment

Online audio – see inside front cover to access.

Edvard Grieg
Arr. by G. E. Holmes

RHYTHM STUDIES

RHYTHM STUDIES

CREATING MUSIC

THEORY

Theme and Variation

Theme and Variation is a technique used by composers and arrangers to create interesting musical ideas that are "varied" from an established melody, or "theme." Play the following theme and two variations to hear how the arranger has created new phrases based on the original melody.

1. THEME

"Simple Gifts"

VARIATION 1 *Adding some notes • Changing some rhythms*

VARIATION 2 *Removing notes • Changing rhythms • Adding accents • Adding notes*

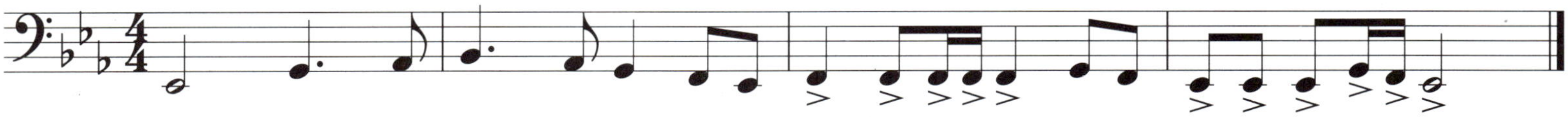

2. THEME AND YOUR VARIATION

Write your own variation of this theme. Use your instrument to hear and try different ideas.

"Candy Mountain Rock"

Theme

Your Variation

THEORY

Blues Improvisation

Improvisation using a **Blues Scale** is an important part of jazz and popular music. Musicians use combinations of these notes and various rhythms to create their own spontaneous solos over a 12 measure progression of chords.

Blues Scale

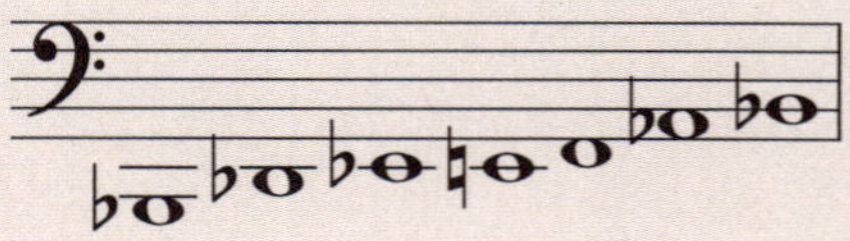

3. LET'S JAM

Use the indicated notes from the Blues Scale to create your own solo to play with the accompaniment (Line B).

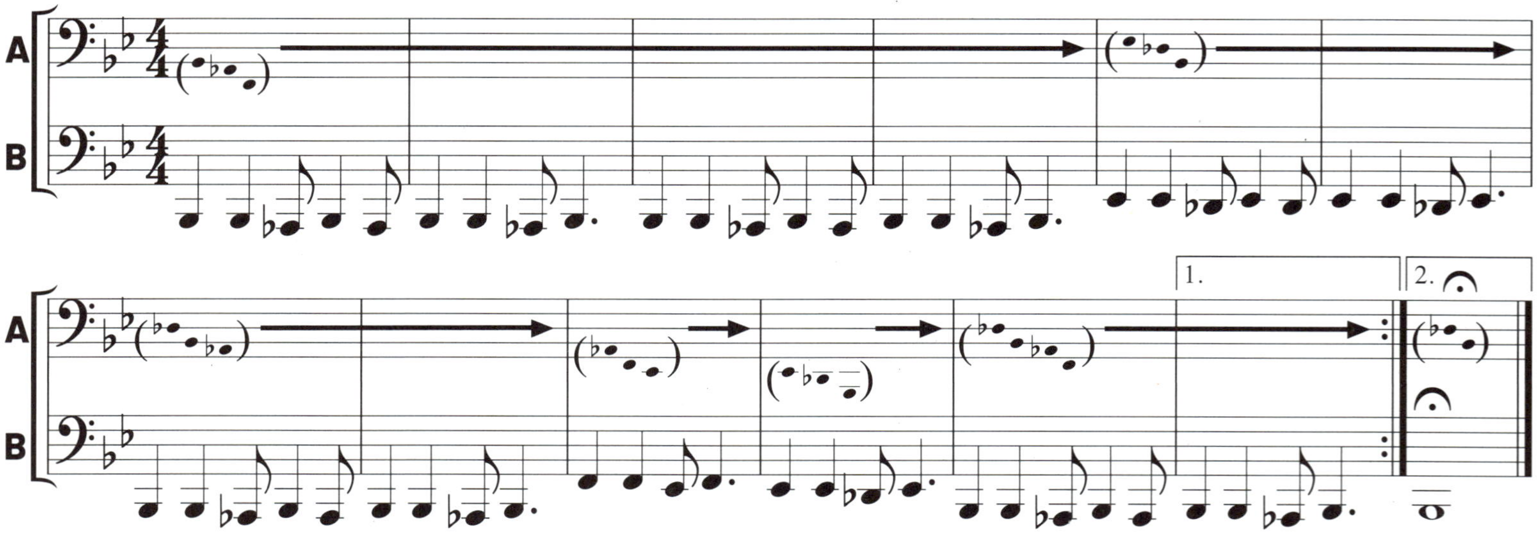

You can mark your progress through the book on this page.
Fill in the stars as instructed by your band director.

1. Page 2–4, Review
2. Page 5, Sightreading Challenge, No. 19
3. Page 6, Daily Warm-Ups
4. Page 7, Sightreading Challenge, No. 31
5. Page 8, Essential Creativity, No. 38
6. Page 9, EE Quiz, No. 43
7. Page 10, Sightreading Challenge, No. 49
8. Page 11, EE Quiz, No. 55
9. Page 12–13, Performance Spotlight
10. Page 15, EE Quiz, No. 74
11. Page 16, Sightreading Challenge, No. 80
12. Page 18, Daily Warm-Ups
13. Page 19, Essential Creativity, No. 96
14. Page 20, Sightreading Challenge, No. 100
15. Page 21, EE Quiz, No. 106
16. Page 22, Chromatic Scale, No. 107
17. Page 23, Sightreading Challenge, No. 115
18. Page 24, EE Quiz, No. 120
19. Page 25, EE Quiz, No. 126
20. Page 27, EE Quiz, No. 133
21. Page 30, Natural Minor Scale, No. 144
22. Page 30, Harmonic Minor Scale, No. 146
23. Page 30, Pomp and Circumstance, No. 148
24. Page 31, Performance Spotlight
25. Page 32, Performance Spotlight
26. Page 33, Performance Spotlight
27. Page 38–39, Individual Study
28. Page 40, Performance Spotlight

MUSIC — AN ESSENTIAL ELEMENT OF LIFE

FINGERING CHART

TUBA

Instrument Care Reminders

Before putting your instrument back in its case after playing, do the following:

- Remove the mouthpiece and wipe it clean. Once a week, wash the mouthpiece with warm tap water. Dry thoroughly.
- Use the water key to empty water from the instrument. Blow air through it.
- Wipe off the instrument with a clean soft cloth. Return the instrument to its case.

Tuba valves occasionally need oiling. To oil your valves, simply:

- Unscrew the valve at the top of the casing.
- Lift the valve half-way out of the casing.
- Apply a few drops of oil to the exposed metal valve.
- Carefully return the valve to its casing. When properly inserted, the top of the valve should easily screw back into place.

Be sure to grease the slides regularly. Your director will recommend special slide grease and valve oil, and will help you apply them when necessary.

CAUTION: If a slide, a valve or your mouthpiece becomes stuck, ask for help from your band director or music dealer. Special tools should be used to prevent damage to your instrument.

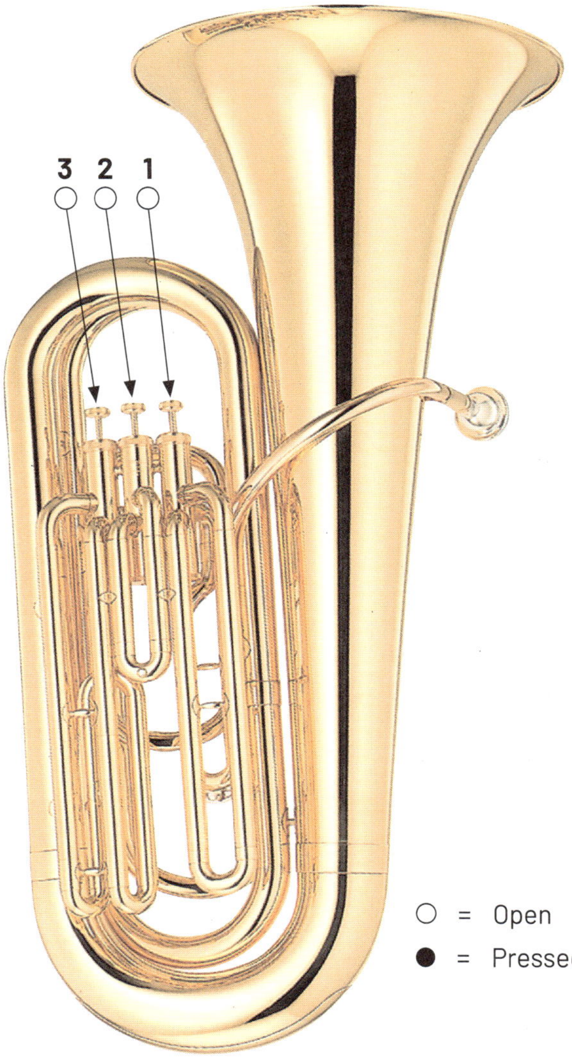

○ = Open

● = Pressed down

Instruments and photos courtesy of Yamaha.

E

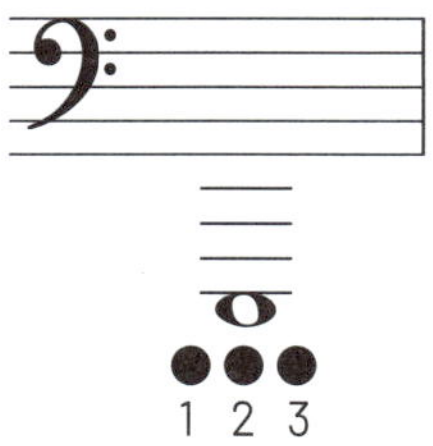

F

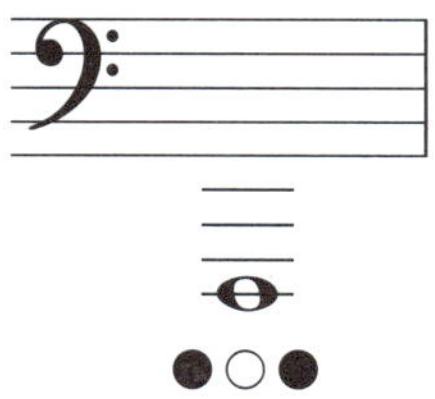

F♯ G♭

G

G♯ A♭

A

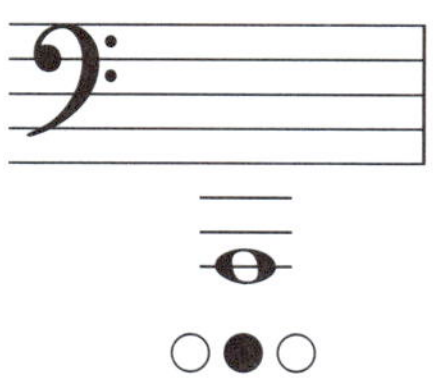

A♯ B♭

B

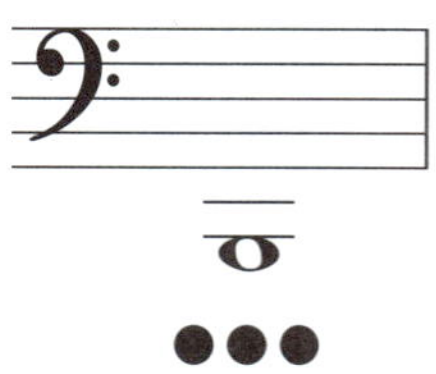

FINGERING CHART

TUBA

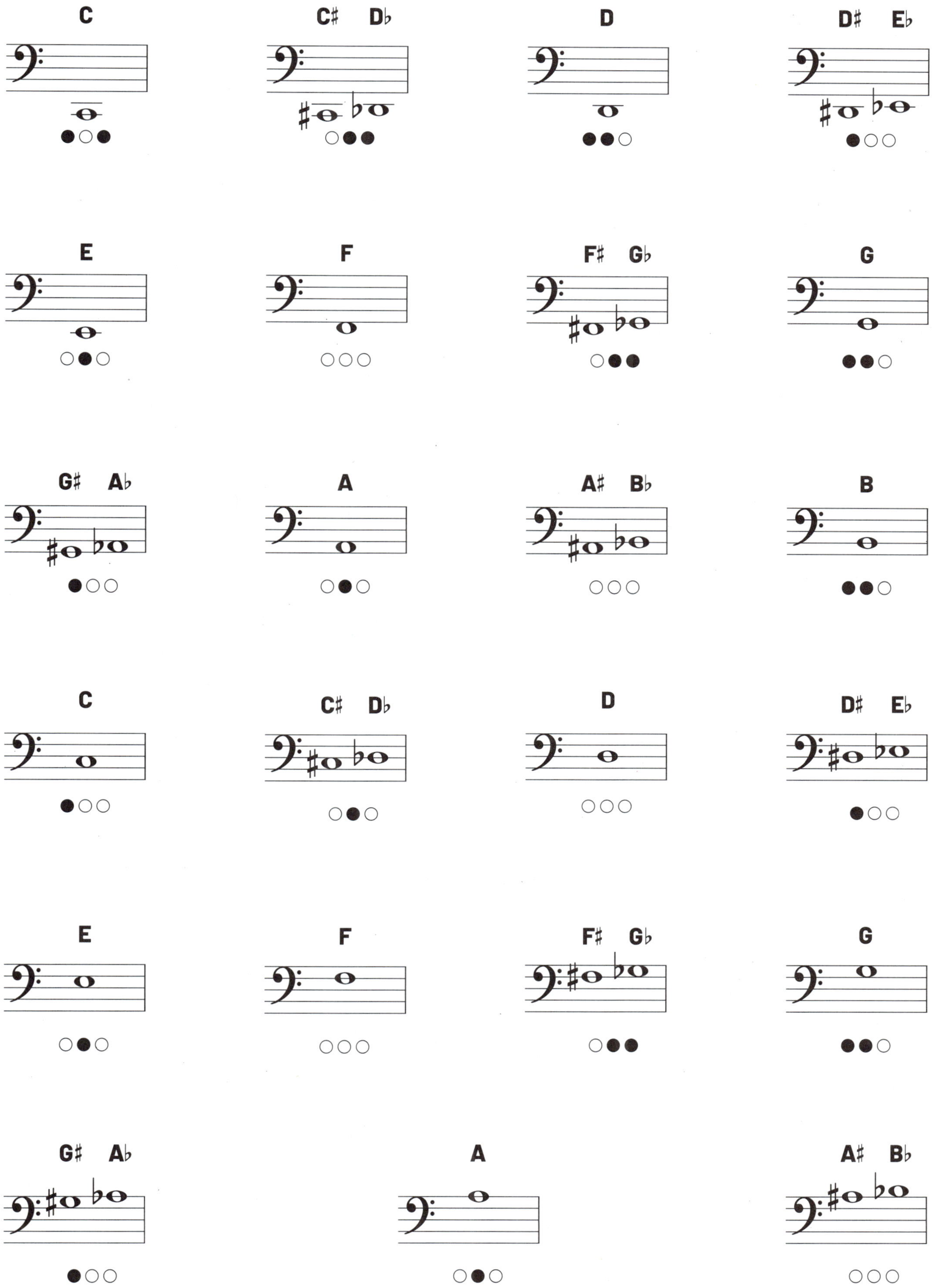

Reference Index

Definitions (pg.)

Book 1 Review

Composers

World Music